A SHARED FUTURE
REDUCING GLOBAL POVERTY

A Statement by the Research and Policy Committee
of the Committee for Economic Development

338.9
C734s

Library of Congress Cataloging-in-Publication Data

Committee for Economic Development. Subcommittee for Globalization.
   A shared future : reducing global poverty : a statement on national policy by the
Research and Policy Committee of the Committee for Economic Development.
      p. cm.
   Includes bibliographical references.
   ISBN 0-87186-145-3
      1. Poverty—Developing countries. 2. Developing countries—Economic policy. 3.
Economic assistance—Developing countries. 4. Economic assistance,
American—Developing countries. I. Committee for Economic Development.
Research and Policy Committee. II. Title.

HC59.72.P6 C66 2002
338.9'009172'4—dc21

                                                    2002067427

First printing in bound-book form: 2002
Paperback: $15.00
Printed in the United States of America
Design: Rowe Design Group

COMMITTEE FOR ECONOMIC DEVELOPMENT
261 Madison Avenue, New York, N.Y. 10016
(212) 688-2063

2000 L Street, N.W., Suite 700, Washington, D.C. 20036
(202) 296-5860

www.ced.org

AHT - 3529

CONTENTS

RESPONSIBILITY FOR CED STATEMENTS ON NATIONAL POLICY

The Committee for Economic Development is an independent research and policy organization of some 250 business leaders and educators. CED is nonprofit, nonpartisan, and nonpolitical. Its purpose is to propose policies that bring about steady economic growth at high employment and reasonably stable prices, increased productivity and living standards, greater and more equal opportunity for every citizen, and an improved quality of life for all.

All CED policy recommendations must have the approval of trustees on the Research and Policy Committee. This committee is directed under the bylaws, which emphasize that "all research is to be thoroughly objective in character, and the approach in each instance is to be from the standpoint of the general welfare and not from that of any special political or economic group." The committee is aided by a Research Advisory Board of leading social scientists and by a small permanent professional staff.

The Research and Policy Committee does not attempt to pass judgment on any pending specific legislative proposals; its purpose is to urge careful consideration of the objectives set forth in this statement and of the best means of accomplishing those objectives.

Each statement is preceded by extensive discussions, meetings, and exchange of memoranda. The research is undertaken by a subcommittee, assisted by advisors chosen for their competence in the field under study.

The full Research and Policy Committee participates in the drafting of recommendations. Likewise, the trustees on the drafting subcommittee vote to approve or disapprove a policy statement, and they share with the Research and Policy Committee the privilege of submitting individual comments for publication.

The recommendations presented herein are those of the trustee members of the Research and Policy Committee and the responsible subcommittee. They are not necessarily endorsed by other trustees or by nontrustee subcommittee members, advisors, contributors, staff members, or others associated with CED.

RESEARCH AND POLICY COMMITTEE

*Voted to approve the policy statement but submitted memoranda of comment, reservation, or dissent. See page 60.

SUBCOMMITTEE ON GLOBALIZATION

---

*Voted to approve the policy statement but submitted memoranda of comment, reservation, or dissent. See page 60.

PURPOSE OF THIS STATEMENT

The September 11 attack against the United States by foreign terrorists illustrates all too clearly the inescapable interconnection between the United States and the rest of the world. More than ever, the United States stands as an example to those around the world who seek prosperity, as well as a target of resentment to those who have not yet achieved it.

As the world's economic powerhouse, the United States and the quality of its leadership have long been under scrutiny. Now, that is even more true. The United States has clear economic, political, and security interests in staying engaged with the world and promoting solutions to global economic problems. In particular, alleviating poverty in developing countries goes beyond humanitarian concerns. It is in our economic interest to expand the markets developing countries provide for our exports and investments, and to realize the saving we achieve by importing from countries that produce goods and services more efficiently. It is in our political interest to encourage a world that is stable, democratic, prosperous, and modern. And it is in our security interest to promote competent, friendly, and stable nations as a means, at a minimum, of reducing armed conflicts around the globe.

Global poverty works against all these goals. Global economic interdependence—the links among nations through trade and investment—is not the problem; it is potentially a major part of the solution to poverty. The challenge to the United States' leadership is to see that that potential is realized. The analysis and recommendations of this report are aimed toward that goal.

ACKNOWLEDGMENTS

This policy statement was developed by the committed and knowledgeable group of business, academic, and policy leaders listed on page vi. We are grateful for the time, efforts, and care that each put into the development of this report.

Special thanks go to the subcommittee co-chairs, Edmund B. Fitzgerald, Managing Director of Woodmont Associates and former Chairman and CEO of Nortel Networks, and Paula Stern, President of The Stern Group, Inc. and former Chair of the U.S. International Trade Commission, for their guidance and leadership. We are also indebted to Elliot Schwartz, Vice President and Director of Economic Studies at CED, Everett Ehrlich, CED's Senior Vice President and Director of Research, and Van Ooms, CED Senior Fellow. Thanks are also due to Isaiah Frank, CED's Advisor on International Economic Policy, for his substantial contributions to this project, and to Tarek Anandan, Michael Berg, and Patricia Loh for research assistance.

Patrick W. Gross, *Co-Chair*
Research and Policy Committee
Founder and Chairman, Executive Committee
American Management Systems, Inc.

Bruce K. MacLaury, *Co-Chair*
Research and Policy Committee
President Emeritus
The Brookings Institution

Chapter 1

SUMMARY, FINDINGS, AND RECOMMENDATIONS

Economic integration through international trade and investment, often characterized as *globalization*, has helped to raise incomes and reduce poverty worldwide. But market forces, although powerful in generating growth, cannot alone generate significant and broad-based reductions in poverty. That will require a concerted effort by both developed and developing countries to create the conditions, institutions, and policies that further economic growth and the sharing of its benefits.

The stake in this effort for low-income countries is clear: absent economic growth, their futures are bleak. Although considerable progress has been made in improving conditions in the world's poorest nations, their populations on average live in poorer health and die significantly earlier than their richer counterparts. The stakes for the United States and other advanced economies, although unchanged, have been made more evident by the September 11 terror attacks and subsequent events. We are now acutely aware that our security, liberty, and prosperity depend on creating a more prosperous and democratic world that rejects backward-looking or terrorist ideologies. It has never been clearer that the United States must provide direction and leadership to build a shared future with the developing world by helping to raise standards of living and reduce poverty globally.

This report is specifically aimed at U.S. and other global business leaders and the governments of countries in which they operate. Our goal is to mobilize their support and recommend steps they can take to help developing countries promote economic growth and reduce poverty. We start from the premise that governments favor economic growth. Not all governments, however, are effectively committed to that goal. Some states lack the basic institutions and political cohesion to govern effectively; others are engaged in external conflicts or internal repression or kleptocracy. To be successful, a country must have the political will to make sustainable economic growth and poverty reduction the highest priorities and to carry out a strategy to that end. Moreover, we recognize, indeed stress, that each country is different and that local conditions, institutions, and policies will primarily decide where and how economic development, income growth, and poverty reduction take place.

Thus the role of business, government leaders, and the public in the advanced economies can only be supportive. They cannot force economic growth on developing countries that do not take the right actions. But without the support of the developed nations, the road to economic advancement for the 85 percent of the world's population who live in developing countries will be much more difficult. Those countries need access to the markets and the financial, managerial, scientific, and technical resources of the more economically developed countries. The transfer of those resources takes place through trade, investment, and development assistance programs. More can be done in each of these areas to improve the economic outlook for the people of developing countries.

1

This CED policy statement explains how business and government can make this outcome more likely.

FINDINGS

Economic development and the reduction of poverty are broad and complex topics that have generated an enormous amount of attention, research, and financial support. On the one hand, the history of the last 50 years is generally encouraging. Poverty is declining, measured both by the number of people and percent of population that are poor. Virtually all regions of the globe have higher incomes today than ever before, and other, non-monetary indicators of human development likewise show significant improvement. On the other hand, economic progress has been disappointing in terms of the severe poverty that continues to exist in a large number of countries, the gap in per capita income between the highest-income and lowest-income countries, and the efforts and resources that have been devoted to closing that gap. A new and revitalized effort is needed. That effort can build on what has been learned:

- Economic growth is essential to the reduction of poverty.

- Countries that successfully open their economies to competition, both domestic and foreign, grow faster than those that do not.

- Policies that support open competition are not sufficient; they must be accompanied by investments in people.

- Countries start with different advantages and disadvantages—some are handicapped by their culture, geography, history, institutions, leadership, or lack of resources—but none are condemned to permanent poverty if they take the steps necessary to promote growth.

The major determinants of economic growth are reasonably well known. Income growth depends on technological advance, the accumulation of capital in all its forms—financial, human, physical, and social—and an institutional and policy framework that uses resources effectively, including the transfer of resources and technology from abroad. The alleviation of poverty generally occurs in tandem with economic growth.

We focus in this statement on a few key policy actions that must be at the core of any development and poverty-reduction strategy:

- setting sound economic policies,

- improving governance and rooting out corruption, and

- investing in human and social capital.

Sound macro and microeconomic policies are necessary for economic development to take root and for progress to be sustained. In general, countries that maintain disciplined budget policies, openness to international trade and investment, and functioning financial markets enjoy stronger long-run economic growth than those that do not. Foreign direct investment in particular brings not only additional financial resources, but also the transfer of modern technology and business methods and wider market opportunities. It also frequently encourages improved labor and environmental practices. Opening the domestic economy to foreign trade and investment can also strengthen competition in domestic markets. Competition leads to a more efficient allocation of resources and provides powerful incentives for productivity growth, which is the source of higher living standards. Establishment of explicit competition policies to prevent anti-competitive practices, similar to U.S. anti-trust policy, would promote this objective.

In many countries a top priority must be effective governance—the development of basic institutional capabilities and establishment of an independent, impartial, and predictable legal system and respect for the rule of law. Developing country governments must put an end to rampant corruption, which drains resources and distorts markets, thereby impairing growth and development. One effective step towards this end would be to operate more openly, subject to scrutiny by an independent judiciary, civil society groups, and a free press. Another would be to eliminate regulations that reduce competition and provide a breeding ground for bribery.

Poverty and underdevelopment are in part a consequence of a lack of education and good health. Investments in these areas, especially when directed at girls and women, generally have very high rates of return and in many cases are preconditions for the success of other economic policies. Foreign direct investment, for example, may have far less impact if not complemented by an educated and healthy labor force. Developing countries should pay special attention to the economic and social benefits of investments in education, health, and social services. In each of these areas governments should include and specifically encourage the participation of women — as a matter of equity, to employ underutilized resources more productively, and to capitalize on the important role women play in effecting social change.

We recognize that these policy directions, although necessary for economic growth, may not in themselves be sufficient to sustain economic development and poverty reduction. There are no "magic bullets." Each country is different and requires unique solutions. The appropriate sequencing and pacing of policy reforms will differ from country to country. However, even countries severely constrained by geography and natural and human resources can benefit from such policy improvements.

RECOMMENDATIONS

In the final analysis, the policies pursued in the developing countries themselves are the key to development. But the advanced economies can make a major contribution to facilitating the development process. Those developing country governments that are pursuing economic growth and poverty reduction generally know what they need to do. The advice they get through both official and private channels, including the World Bank, regional development banks, bilateral aid agencies like the U.S. Agency for International Development (USAID), private investors, and non-governmental organizations, is fairly consistent on the main points. For various reasons, however, some governments are reluctant to take the actions needed for economic advancement. The advanced economies also often appear hesitant about taking actions that could help developing countries.

Our recommendations clarify the actions that governments and businesses in the advanced economies can take to help developing countries help themselves. These actions are not entirely altruistic; they will also benefit the advanced economies. The most important step would be to remove the tariffs, quotas, and subsidies that impede developing country exports. The second would be to support developing country efforts to establish domestic conditions that attract foreign direct investment. A third would be to increase official development assistance and, especially, to manage it more effectively by improving its allocation, its delivery, and the measurement of its impact on development and poverty reduction.

Building U.S. Leadership for A Global Attack on Poverty

A key missing ingredient in the United States and some other advanced economies is public and private support for policies that would help developing countries help themselves. Support lags in part because the public lacks sufficient knowledge of conditions in developing countries and of policies and programs in their own country that affect economic development. For example, surveys show that the U.S. public consistently overestimates the amount of government resources devoted to foreign aid (official development assistance) and undervalues the benefits of open markets for trade and investment. We therefore recommend the following:

- **Leaders of global business, educational, and social institutions should rally public and private support for a strategy to overcome global poverty.* They should articulate a new vision of global cooperation based on**

  - **reforms in developing countries that will maintain sound economic policies, improve governance and eradicate corruption, and invest in education, health, and other forms of human development; and**

  - **reforms in developed countries to eliminate trade distortions, support foreign direct investment, and increase and better manage official development assistance.**

A diverse group of educational and social organizations are already involved in seeking solutions to problems that plague developing countries. Some, such as the Global Business Council on HIV/AIDS and the World Economic Forum's Global Health Initiative, work predominately with business executives, corporations, and other non-profit organizations, while others may be more broadly based or affiliated with religious, educational, or other social organizations. Such organizations are important resources for rallying public opinion and effecting change.

- **Business leaders and their employees should become involved in the leading educational and social organizations that are promoting constructive solutions to the economic, health, and social problems of low-income countries.***

We are encouraged by the increased cooperation between developed and developing countries made possible by public-private partnerships, which provide a framework for mobilizing the skills and resources of the private sector in advanced economies to provide higher quality and more efficient public services in developing countries.

- **We support the formation of public-private partnerships in developing countries to achieve carefully articulated and specific outcomes, such as building institutional capabilities, transferring technical expertise, and delivering critical services.**

Opening Markets for Trade and Investment

Sound policies in developing countries should be complemented by pro-development economic policies in developed countries.

Trade

The World Bank estimates that abolishing trade restrictions in both developing and developed countries could boost income in the developing countries by $1.5 trillion over ten years; incomes in developed countries could rise by a like amount, with Western Europe's consumers and taxpayers benefiting most from the elimination of heavy subsidies for domestic agriculture. The constant drumbeat of advice from the advanced economies, aid agencies, and the International Monetary Fund for developing countries to open their economies to trade must be backed up by like reforms in the United States, the European Union, and Japan.

*See memoranda by THOMAS J. BUCKHOLTZ (page 60).

- **The United States and other developed countries should reduce trade barriers to developing country products and services.*** **The United States should take the lead in the World Trade Organization (WTO) to ensure that developing countries have access to developed country markets. It should seek to speed up the implementation of tariff reductions under the** *Agreement on Textiles and Clothing* **(which replaced the** *Multi-Fiber Arrangement***) and tighten WTO rules on anti-dumping so that only the most worthy complaints would qualify for protection. Production subsidies for domestic agriculture, which are especially heavy in the European Union and Japan, should also be eliminated.**

We recognize that there is strong domestic opposition to such market-opening measures. We urge, as in previous policy statements, that policy makers explicitly address worker anxieties about job displacement.

- **In conjunction with reducing trade barriers and tightening standards for anti-dumping actions, the United States should bolster its system of adjustment assistance. As part of this effort, it should adopt a limited system of wage and health insurance for displaced workers.***

Investment

We encourage developing countries to make the attraction of foreign direct investment one of their highest development priorities. For the most part, developed economies impose few restrictions (mostly related to national security) on outward investments. But there are actions that developed country governments and businesses can take to help developing countries to attract foreign capital. For example, multinational corporations can do more to advance

ethical standards, employ more transparent reporting practices, and ensure that the supply side of bribery payments is closed, which would have direct benefits for the corporation and in some countries could change the atmosphere of corruption. In addition, the U.S. government should take the lead in promoting a multilateral investment agreement that would create common rules for the treatment of direct investments. Such an agreement would reduce risks, reassure investors, and make it easier for them to take equity positions in developing countries.

- **All countries should ratify the OECD** *Anti-Bribery Convention* **and fully prosecute under national laws the illegal payment of bribes. CED urges multinational corporations to abide by internationally recognized standards of integrity and consider implementing voluntary reporting practices that make public the impact of their activities on the domestic economy. They should also comply with relevant OECD conventions and other appropriate international codes against bribery and corruption.**

- **The United States should push to extend the WTO's** *Agreement on Trade-Related Investment Measures* **(TRIMs) into a more effective multilateral investment code. The primary goal of such a code should be to create a common set of rules for the national treatment of foreign direct investment. In addition, countries should agree to report publicly their use of special incentives to attract investment, such as tax abatements and other financial inducements, and submit them to review by the WTO. Such transparency could help rein in the use of such incentives by all WTO members and discourage policies that might reduce labor and environmental standards to attract foreign investment.**

---

*See memoranda by PETER A. BENOLIEL (page 60).

Beyond Open Markets: Investing in Education And Health

Many developing country governments give inadequate support to public education and health care. Some countries undervalue the economic returns from such investments in human capital. In many cases, however, the meager support is simply due to a lack of financial resources. Investments in basic education, health, and nutrition enhance not only the productive capacity of individuals, but also that of the whole economy. Governments do not have an exclusive role in these investments; multinational corporations can improve the productivity of their labor forces by providing training and health services to their employees.

- **We encourage all relevant public and private organizations to contribute to the improvement of education and health outcomes in developing countries. Developing country governments should make it one of their top priorities to improve the delivery and quality of education and health services. Similarly, developed country governments should focus attention and development assistance funding on improving education and health, especially in the poorest countries. In addition, we encourage multinational corporations, as employers, to provide appropriate education, training, and health services for their employees.**

- **In each of these endeavors, special attention and resources should be dedicated to improving the status of women: investments in the education and health of women have high social rates of return because of their work and family roles. Similarly, development programs that assist small businesses, farmers, and other commercial ventures should recognize the unique contributions of women.**

Development Assistance

Trade and investment provide the bulk of the resources that flow from the developed to the developing world. But, development assistance often provides an important supplement. For the least developed nations, it can be a major resource, sometimes accounting for more than 100 percent of gross capital formation. Where a country is pursuing sound economic policies, development aid can "fill the gap" by providing critical resources until the country can achieve sufficient domestic savings, access to international capital markets, and foreign direct investment to meet its investment needs.

Development aid works most effectively when it reinforces good local policies by rewarding effective performance. A recent UN conference on *Financing for Development* discussed the level of aid from donor countries, how aid should be given, and whether the funding of aid should be more automatic. Some business and national leaders have called for a doubling of aid and for automatic financing mechanisms, such as a tax on financial transactions, to fund development programs. Others have proposed a "common pool" approach to aid delivery, which would put more authority and responsibility in the hands of recipient countries.

Although we have concerns about how aid has been allocated and managed in the past, a strong case for more development aid can be made on both economic and humanitarian grounds and to strengthen U.S. leadership in policy engagement with developing countries. But, setting an arbitrary financing goal, such as a specified percentage of Gross Domestic Product (GDP), as has been the practice, inverts the logic of financial decisionmaking. The rationale for increased development assistance must be its effectiveness, not an aggregate target. We should not invest scarce resources that have little return nor hesitate to increase spending where it will be effective.

In this regard, our views are consistent with President Bush's proposal for a new Millennium Challenge Account within the U.S. foreign aid budget. As outlined, countries that improve governance and root out corruption, encourage economic freedom through sound economic policies, and invest in their people, would receive more aid from the United States. Aid would increase over the next three years by $5 billion, resulting in an annual level of about $15 billion, and would be linked to measurable improvements in performance. These new resources would be allocated to countries that are undertaking sound economic reforms and would be concentrated in areas such as health and education, where the case for support is clear because the activities are more often programmatically sound, with measurable results. CED supports this proposal and would support shifting even more of the U.S. foreign aid budget to this account and, if successful, adding more funds.

- **Donors should provide increases in official development assistance as long as they are confident that such aid can be spent effectively. The allocation of aid should be based on the soundness of a country's development policies and on measurable improvements in specific areas such as education and health, rather than on pre-determined country allotments. To measure the effectiveness of increased spending, more resources should be devoted to improving the collection, dissemination, and use of data on conditions in developing countries. We do not support schemes for automatic funding of aid programs through international taxes or other financing mechanisms that skirt the normal appropriations process.**

Chapter 2
INTRODUCTION: ECONOMIC INTEGRATION AND POVERTY REDUCTION

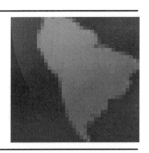

The increased integration of markets around the world—a process often referred to as globalization—has increased the efficiency of resource use, widened choices available to consumers, and boosted incomes. Some of the technological and economic factors that underlie this market integration are almost certain to continue, such as the increased speed, greater capabilities, and lower costs of transportation, communication, and information. However, the continuation of other factors, the most important being efforts by developing country governments to build the capabilities of their domestic institutions and to lower barriers to foreign trade and investment, are much less certain. A clear and convincing case exists for further market-opening policies in both developing and developed countries. Yet, in many places, including the United States, the issue seems in doubt.

The doubt stems in part from both misunderstanding and basic politics. Far from contributing to global poverty, open foreign trade and direct investment are part of the solution to it. Without the growth related to economic integration, developing countries will be unable to raise incomes and sustain poverty-reduction strategies. Developed countries, such as the United States, must understand that the rationale for economic integration is mutual benefit. Increased trade with, and higher incomes in, the developing countries add to our prosperity and security. Protectionist policies not only make the United States poorer, but also undercut growth in the developing countries and make the rhetoric of open markets hollow.

Yielding to protectionism creates temporary help for those directly challenged by imports, but at high costs to others. Rather than imposing restraints on trade, as was recently done for steel products, direct adjustment programs can address the legitimate concerns of those who bear the costs of economic change, without imposing hidden costs. A well-crafted adjustment program ought to provide assistance more effectively and efficiently than trade protection.

The multinational corporation (MNC) can play a significant role in overcoming the misunderstandings that accompany economic integration. In many respects the MNC is the transmission belt for information, resources, and political leadership in the global economy. Many of the recommendations of this report urge the leaders of global companies to take a more active role in improving public knowledge and awareness of the global economy in both developing and developed countries and to lend the weight of their support to sound economic and social policies.

OPEN MARKETS FOSTER ECONOMIC GROWTH

Economies that remain closed to international trade and investment cannot benefit from the efficiencies of the global marketplace. Likewise, governments that fail to provide the basic institutional foundation for economic growth, including respect for the rule of law, effectively shut off their access to the world economy's resources. The countries that have grown the fastest and made the most progress in reducing poverty are those that have chosen to take advantage of the opportunities offered in the global economy. That does not mean that dysfunctional government policy is the sole cause of poverty or that a change in economic policy will produce rapid prosperity. Culture, politics, and religion all shape a society and circumscribe its economic outcomes. Nevertheless, without government policies that support sustainable economic growth, the reduction of poverty will be much more difficult, if not doomed to failure.

A Focus on Poverty

The gaps in incomes and living conditions between the high-income and low-income countries and the extent of absolute poverty are unacceptable. In addition to raising humanitarian concerns, such large disparities undermine the social consensus essential for global political stability. A recent report of the Commission on U.S. National Security in the 21st Century recognizes the danger of poverty in developing countries. It concludes: "It is a significant national interest of the United States that there be economic growth abroad, to raise living standards of the poorest and to mitigate economic and political conflict."[1] As stated by President Bush, "poverty prevents governments from controlling their borders, policing their territory, and enforcing their laws. Development provides the resources to build hope and prosperity, and security."[2]

The existence of extreme poverty in developing countries, although not caused by market-opening policies, fuels an anti-globalization and anti-American backlash. To garner support, globalization must be inclusive. It must demonstrate that it serves the broadest possible collection of countries and people, not just the interests of the United States and other advanced economies or the elites in developing countries. In fact, U.S. interests—

economic, political, security, and humanitarian—cannot be met unless economic conditions in nations with substantial populations in poverty improve.

Economic development, supported by globalization, holds the promise of raising incomes and significantly improving the material conditions in which people live. Research confirms that economic growth and poverty reduction go hand-in-hand.[3] Without economic growth, poverty can be reduced only by redistributing income or wealth: a politically tortuous process. In the long run, excessive redistribution policies can impede growth by reducing incentives. In the final analysis, reducing poverty means raising productivity. Higher productivity—output per unit of input—raises incomes; as incomes rise poverty declines. Increases in productivity are generated by improvements in the quality of human and physical resources and the efficiency with which those resources are transformed into products and services. Advances in technology, including improvement in the management of enterprises, are the key.

Productivity increases often require investment, which requires domestic savings. However, domestic resources can be supplemented through foreign trade and investment. Foreign trade and investment reduce gaps in knowledge and resources that separate low-productivity and, hence, low-income countries from high-productivity and high-income countries. Such economic integration also brings greater exposure to enlightened thinking and practices, such as the desirability of educating women, that can help break down customs and practices that hold people in poverty. States that have embraced globalization by liberalizing rules for trade and investment and putting in place sound domestic institutions and policies have grown substantially faster than those that have rejected such a course. By one estimate, the number of absolute poor in developing countries that have embraced globalization declined by 120 million between 1993 and 1998, while poverty increased in other developing countries by 20 million.[4] Although in some cases the gap between rich and poor in individual countries may widen, research has found no systematic relationship between income inequality and either globalization or economic growth.[5]

Open markets, however, are not by themselves sufficient to eliminate poverty. Complementary policies and institutions are also needed. Investing in education and health, for example, ameliorates harsh conditions, improves the quality of the workforce, and widens opportunities for the poor. Many of the deprivations associated with poverty, such as premature mortality, significant undernourishment (especially of children), persistent morbidity, widespread illiteracy, and other failures diminish productivity and make escape from poverty difficult.[6] In addition to opening markets and investing a high percentage of GDP, countries that have achieved high rates of economic growth and poverty reduction have maintained macroeconomic stability, stabilized political institutions, and invested in human resources.[7]

Historical Background

Viewed from a historical perspective, poverty is declining. Virtually all regions of the globe have higher incomes today than ever before, and the percentage of people in absolute poverty has never been lower. Indicators of human development such as average longevity and literacy are higher; infant mortality has declined significantly. (See Table 1)

From 1950-1973, the world saw unprecedented productivity and income growth. The average annual compound rate of growth in per capita income worldwide during that period was a remarkable 2.9 percent, high by historical standards.[8] Global growth slowed after 1973, but with the exceptions of Eastern Europe and Africa, per capita income has

Table 1

Global Progress in Economic and Human Development, 1950-1999

Indicator	1950	1998 or 1999
Average income per capita (1990 dollars)[a]		
World	2,114	5,709
Developing countries	1,093	3,102
Average longevity (years)		
World	49	66
Developing countries	44	64
Share of population living on less than $2 a day (percent)		
World	63	40[b]
Developing countries	n.a.	n.a.
Share of population living on less than $1 a day (percent)		
World	42	17[b]
Developing countries	n.a.	26
Share of population literate (percent)		
World	54	79
Developing countries	40	75
Infant mortality (deaths per 1,000 live births)		
World	156[c]	54
Developing countries	179[c]	59

a. At purchasing power parity.
b. In 1992.
c. In 1950-55.

SOURCE: United Nations, *Report of the High-Level Panel on Financing for Development,* June 2000, Annex.

continued to rise. Living standards have risen far more in some countries than in others, but much of the difference can be accounted for by policy interventions in both the developing and developed countries. South Korea, for example, experienced 6.6 percent average annual growth in per capita GDP between 1965 and 1999. China and Singapore averaged 6.4 and 6.3 percent annual growth in per capita GDP, respectively, over the same period. However, during the same period, average incomes in sub-Saharan Africa fell by 0.2 percent annually.[9]

The 155 middle- and low-income nations, often collectively described as "developing countries," comprise a highly diverse group. (See Table 2) Their average incomes range from less than $755 per year (63 countries) to over $2,996 and as much as $9,265 (38 countries). Their prospects differ. Some are land locked and have very few domestic resources to develop. Others have substantial economic potential but lack the political and social institutions to support economic advancement. The fastest growing countries are those that have economic and political policies that support entrepreneurship.

CURRENT EFFORTS TO REDUCE POVERTY

The International Development Goals are a set of indicators used to quantify and assess the progress of the international efforts to reduce poverty. The OECD Development Assistance Committee (DAC) in its 1996 report, *Shaping the 21st Century*, first set out the goals, but they are derived from previous agreements and resolutions made at United Nations conferences on education, children, the environment, human rights, and women during the early 1990's. The goals are nearly identical to the Millennium Development Goals, which were announced at the U.N.

Millennium Summit in September 2000. They primarily address four facets of poverty: extremely low income, lack of education, inadequate health, and environmental degradation. (See Box, The International Development Goals) The goals seek to create a small number of measurable outcomes to facilitate setting priorities and to foster public support for providing the resources necessary to achieve them.

The development goals are a useful starting point for addressing poverty. They help focus attention on the problems of developing countries and their progress in meeting specific benchmarks. Numeric goals have led the United Nations and specialized international agencies to put greater effort into measuring and monitoring the many dimensions of poverty.[10] Increased efforts have also gone into surveying household income, living standards, and health status. More such information is needed.

However, it is difficult to make these development goals operational. The specificity of the goals contrasts with the lack of specific accountability and operational guidance. For example, does the goal of halving poverty apply to poor people generally or to each country individually? Who is responsible for achieving the goal? How is the reduction of poverty to be accomplished?

The most prominent goal is to reduce by half the proportion of people living in extreme poverty, with income less than one dollar per day, by 2015.[†] Viewed globally, progress towards the goal is being made. Nearly 1.2 billion people, 23.4 percent of world population, were estimated to have income of less than a dollar a day in 1998,

Table 2

World Bank Country Classification Scheme

Country Income Classification	Number of Countries	GNI/ Capita Range[a]	Average GNI/ Capita[a]
High Income		$9266 or more	
OECD	23		27,857
Non-OECD	29		18,906
Middle Income			
Upper Middle	38	$2996-$9265	4,360
Lower Middle	54	$756 -$2995	1,032
Low Income	63	$755 or less	418

a. 1999 US$

SOURCE: World Bank, *World Development Indicators Database.*

---

† The baseline year for the targets is 1990, which has been consistently used by the global conferences of the past decade. The international poverty line was set at $1/day in 1985 purchasing power parity (PPP) terms to take into account the local prices of goods and services and a more realistic cost of living. It has been recalculated in 1993 PPP terms at about $1.08 a day.

a significant reduction in the poverty rate from 28.9 percent in 1990. However, progress is very uneven. Because total population in developing countries has increased by about 600 million, the actual number of people living on less than one dollar a day has dropped only by about 100 million. Moreover, if the poverty level is defined at two dollars a day, the number of people in poverty jumps to 2.8 billion, nearly half the world's population and a slight rise since 1990.

Much of the progress has come in the East Asia and Pacific region, in particular in China where the absolute number of people living

THE INTERNATIONAL DEVELOPMENT GOALS

The International Development Goals (IDGs) are designed to reduce poverty, improve global health and education levels, and protect the environment. In general, the goals are set for 2015: the reference point, or base year, is 1990.

The seven International Development Goals are:

- Reduce Extreme Poverty
- Facilitate Universal Primary Education
- Promote Gender Equality
- Reduce Child Mortality
- Improve Maternal Health
- Combat HIV/AIDS and other Infectious Diseases
- Ensure Environmental Sustainability

POVERTY REDUCTION

- *Reduce the proportion of people living in extreme poverty by at least one-half by 2015.*

Extreme poverty is defined as income less than one dollar per day. Although poverty reduction is explicitly addressed only with this goal, all the goals — such as improving a country's health, education, and environmental conditions — help reduce poverty.

EDUCATION

- *All countries should have universal primary education.*
- *Gender disparity in primary and secondary education should be eliminated by 2005.*

Enrollment. Although worldwide primary school enrollment rates are increasing, over 113 million school-aged children are estimated to be out of school.[11] Enrollment rates vary significantly within countries (as a result of income and wealth differences), between countries, and between regions, and differences in population growth rates and resources available for education have the potential to increase educational disparities over the next decade. The percentage of children not enrolled in school ranges from a low of 3 percent in East Asia to over 40 percent in sub-Saharan Africa.

While an important indicator, enrollment rates may not measure education outcomes. Many children who are legitimately enrolled in school may not actually attain basic skills.

Gender Equality. Nearly 60 percent of uneducated school-aged children are girls, and girls are less likely to complete their basic education than their male counterparts. In some cases, girls are kept out of school as a result of religious or social practices. In other cases, they, or in poverty was reduced by nearly 150 million despite population growth of over 100 million.[12] (See Table 3) The Republic of Korea, Malaysia, and Morocco have been able to reduce the number of people living in poverty by half in less than a generation.[13] Progress has also been made in Latin America and the Caribbean, where the annual rate of poverty reduction is above that necessary to meet the goal by 2015. Other regions face a far more formidable task. The percentage of people living in absolute poverty is approaching 50 percent in the 48 countries of sub-Saharan Africa and remains around 40 percent in the

their families, may be discouraged because of the limited employment opportunities for educated women in many developing nations.

Aside from the direct benefits to women from education, gender equality in schools is important to development because educated women tend to have smaller, healthier families and provide better care for their children. Incomes of families with educated women are generally higher, and educated women are much more likely to encourage their children to be educated as well. In most societies women are important agents of cultural change. Societies that promote the education of women are also more likely to embrace other cultural changes that promote economic development.

HEALTH

- *Reduce the death rates for infants and children under the age of five years by two-thirds.*

- *Reduce the rate of maternal mortality by three-fourths.*

- *All individuals of appropriate ages should have access through the primary health-care system to reproductive health services.*

A population with a high number of infant, child, and maternal deaths, is an unproductive population that is incapable of escaping poverty. 11 million children under the age of five died in 1998. More than a half-million women die each year during pregnancy and childbirth.[14] HIV/AIDS killed 3 million people in 2001, bringing the world total to over 20 million since the beginning of the epidemic in the late 1970s.[15] Infant and maternal fatalities and deaths from infectious diseases are preventable, but most developing countries devote insufficient resources to these concerns. Improved reproductive health services would have many benefits, including the slowing of world population growth, the fighting of infectious diseases including HIV/AIDS, malaria, and tuberculosis, and the education of people to help them live healthier lives.

ENVIRONMENTAL SUSTAINABILITY

- *Every country should have a current national strategy for sustainable development, in the process of implementation, by 2005.*

The world's most impoverished people are disproportionately affected by environmental degradation, such as desertification, land degradation, water scarcity, and natural disasters. About 5 million people in developing countries die from waterborne diseases and polluted air every year.[16]

Economic development has the potential in the short run to lead to greater environmental degradation, both through the overuse of resources and the creation of damaging by-products. However, studies have shown that as national income rises, more resources are usually dedicated to environmental cleanup and preservation.

Table 3

Progress Towards The Achievement of Poverty Reduction Goals[a]

Region	1990			1998			2015			Reduction Rates	
	Population (millions)	<$1/day (millions)	% in Poverty	Population (millions)	<$1/day (millions)	% in Poverty	Projected Population (millions)	Goal < $1/day (millons)	Goal % in Poverty	Annual Rate of Change in Poverty (in percents) 1990-1998	Annual Poverty Rate Reduction Necessary to Meet Goal (in percents)
East Asia & Pacific	1,638.7	452.4	27.6	1,816.6	267.1	14.7	2,097	289.5	13.8	7.6	0.4
Europe & Central Asia	466.1	7.1	1.5	473.9	17.6	3.7	478	3.6	0.8	-11.8	8.9
Latin America & Caribbean	438.2	73.8	16.8	500.3	60.7	12.1	622	52.3	8.4	4.0	2.1
Middle East & North Africa	237.8	5.7	2.4	284.4	6.0	2.1	390	4.7	1.2	1.6	3.3
South Asia	1,122.1	495.1	44.1	1,304.6	521.8	40.0	1,676	369.8	22.1	1.2	3.4
Sub-Saharan Africa	508.0	242.3	47.7	626.9	301.6	48.1	878	209.4	23.8	-0.1	4.0
Total	**4,411.0**	**1,276.4**	**28.9**	**5,006.7**	**1,174.8**	**23.5**	**6,141**	**888.5**	**14.5**	**2.6**	**2.8**

a. Table excludes populations of high-income countries.

SOURCES: World Bank, *World Development Indicators Database*, and World Bank, *World Development Indicators*, 2001.

eight South Asian countries. Many countries will fall far short of meeting this development goal if the recent pace of change continues.

As a result of low economic and high population growth rates, sub-Saharan Africa has the largest share of people living below one dollar a day. Consequently, a great deal of international effort has been focused on the African countries. Traditionally, such efforts have taken the form of official development assistance, but in recent years the advanced economies have focused on other types of assistance, including debt reduction through the Heavily Indebted Poor Countries (HIPC) Initiative and increased market access. Europe and the United States have provided trade preferences to African products through the *Cotonou Partnership Agreement* and African Growth and Opportunity Act, respectively. Business leaders have formed the Corporate Council on Africa, a non-profit organization that seeks to raise the profile of Africa in the U.S. business community, there-

by strengthening and facilitating commercial relationships between the United States and the African continent.[17]

African governments are well aware that their own efforts to liberalize and reform are crucial. With the assistance of the World Bank and IMF, many African nations have completed Poverty Reduction Strategy Papers, which are required of countries that want to participate in the HIPC initiative. In the past year, African leaders have come together to form the New Partnership for Africa's Development (NEPAD) to accomplish their pledge to eradicate poverty and increase growth in their nations. Through NEPAD, the Africans have committed themselves to a broad range of measures to improve local infrastructure, promote the private sector and regional integration, enhance good governance, and improve the local investment climate. While the success of the program will depend on the ability of the group to create concrete regional cooperation projects, the partnership is an important sign that African leaders and governments are committed and determined to take charge of their futures.

THE NEED FOR A LONG-TERM PERSPECTIVE, REALISTIC EXPECTATIONS, AND PROMPT ACTION

Ending or significantly reducing poverty is a long-term goal. Even at relatively high rates of growth in GDP, economic development and the benefits of higher income growth take time to materialize. Nevertheless, success can be achieved and immediate actions can have high payoffs. In China, per capita income on a purchasing-power-parity basis has grown from $270 in 1975 to $3940 in 2000.[18]

To illustrate the prospects for poverty reduction, the World Bank has calculated the results of three alternative scenarios.[19][†] In the base case, which is now probably beyond reach, the world as a whole would reach the international development goal of reducing the share of people living on less than one dollar per day by 2015 to half of what it was in 1990. (See Table 4) That scenario would still leave the total number of absolute poor at near 800 million, and the number of poor would continue to grow in sub-Saharan Africa. Under a middle scenario of relatively low growth, only East Asia would be able to meet the poverty reduction target. The total number of poor in the world would be above 1 billion. Excluding China it would remain largely unchanged from the 1990 level. A lower-growth scenario, roughly equivalent to the average rate of growth during the 1990s (about 1.7 percent), leaves the number in poverty only marginally lower than in 1998, just under 1.2 billion.

[†] These scenarios were prepared before the September 11 attacks on the United States, and therefore do not take into account the resulting slowdown in world economic activity since then.

Table 4		
Poverty in Developing Countries under Alternative Scenarios		
	$1 a day	
	Headcount ratio (percent)	Number of poor (million)
1990	29.0	1,276
1998	23.4	1,175
2015: base case scenario	12.6	777
2015: low growth scenario	16.4	1,011
2015: growth as in 1990s	18.7	1,157

Base case = real per capita GDP growth in developing countries of 3.5-4.0 percent annually.
Low growth case = real per capita GDP growth in developing countries of about 2.5 percent annually.
1990s growth case = real per capita GDP growth in developing countries of about 1.7 percent annually.

SOURCE: World Bank, *Global Economic Prospects*, 2001.

In each case, the percentage of population in poverty declines. However, because of continuing population growth, slower economic growth leaves the number of people in poverty at very high levels. Most important, over this 15-year period a difference of about one percentage point in per capita income growth has very large effects on outcomes. The regional and country-specific variations implied by these scenarios are also quite large. In Africa, the number of people living in poverty would increase under all scenarios.

THE NEED FOR LEADERSHIP AND SUPPORT FROM DEVELOPED COUNTRIES

For the developing countries, the path to economic growth is reasonably clear. For those inclined to listen, the advice from international institutions and governments of the advanced economies is consistent on the main points. Although developing country governments have the primary responsibility for carrying out policies that promote economic growth and poverty reduction, they are not completely masters of their own fates. They need the advanced economies to remove trade distortions that hinder developing country exports, continue to supply privately financed transfers of capital and technical expertise, and support increased and more effective publicly financed development aid.

Support from the United States and some other advanced economies for policies that would help developing countries to help themselves lags in part because the public does not comprehended the relationship between the needs of the developing countries and their own interests. Since the terror attacks on the United States, that may have begun to change, as news reports and media coverage of international conditions have increased. But the public still does not have sufficient knowledge of developing countries and our relations with them. Many are unaware of how policies and programs in the advanced economies affect the developing countries. For example, surveys show that the U.S. public consistently overestimates the amount of government resources devoted to foreign aid (official development assistance), and under values the net benefits of open markets for trade and investment.[20] Thus, we recommend the following:

- **Leaders of global business, educational, and social institutions should rally public and private support for a strategy to overcome global poverty. They should articulate a new vision of global cooperation based on**

    - **reforms in developing countries that will maintain sound economic policies, improve governance and eradicate corruption, and invest in education, health, and other forms of human development; and**

    - **reforms in developed countries to eliminate trade distortions, support foreign direct investment, and increase and better manage official development assistance.**

A diverse group of educational and social organizations is already involved in seeking solutions to problems that plague developing countries. Some, such as the Global Business Council on HIV/AIDS and the World Economic Forum's Global Health Initiative, work predominantly with business executives, corporations, and other non-profit organizations, while others may be more broadly based or affiliated with religious, educational, or other social organizations. Such organizations are important resources for rallying public opinion and effecting change. **Business leaders and their employees should become involved in the leading educational and social organizations that are promoting constructive solutions to the economic, health, and social problems of low-income countries.**

A promising step toward the efficient and speedy delivery of critical services to the poor and improved cooperation between developing and developed countries is the trend toward public-private partnerships. Such partnerships bring together the private sector's ability to implement projects quickly and efficiently with the public sector's responsibility in the host country to establish both its own priorities and the ground rules under which the private sector will operate and be paid.

Public-private partnerships can help even the world's poorest countries, where governments and people are too poor to pay for all the critical water, power, transportation, health, and other infrastructure facilities they need. In these countries, the private sector could take the lead in developing, financing, implementing, and operating projects deemed to be of the highest priority by the governments of the recipient countries and by Western donor countries. Western donor countries and institutions could pay in whole or in part for the services provided by these projects through an agreed upon schedule based on services delivered. This would provide a strong incentive for efficient service delivery.

Placing the responsibility for implementation of these projects (and the flow of funds for these projects) in the private sector would help assure that needed projects would be implemented quickly, efficiently, and transparently, with much less potential for corrupt diversion of funds. Thus, it would help address some of the key criticisms leveled against foreign aid in the United States and elsewhere.

In partnerships, the skills and assets of the public and private sectors are shared in delivering a product or service to the public. In addition to sharing resources, the groups share the potential risks and rewards of the project. Therefore, each party maintains an influence on the objectives and operations of the partnership and is responsible for ensuring the delivery of the good or service.

This "joint ownership" feature helps to distinguish partnerships from ordinary contracting and privatization programs on the one hand and private philanthropy on the other. Although public-private partnerships are defined by their joint ownership, they exist in several different forms and have been formed in many different sectors, including health, education, transportation, defense, information technology, and environmental protection.[21] (Examples of different public-private partnerships are highlighted where relevant in subsequent chapters.)

We support the formation of public-private partnerships in developing countries to achieve carefully articulated and specific outcomes, such as building institutional capabilities, transferring technical expertise, and delivering critical services.

Chapter 3

THE NEED FOR POLITICAL LEADERSHIP AND INSTITUTION-BUILDING IN DEVELOPING COUNTRIES

We start with the assumption that a developing country's government and societal leaders are committed to the goal of economic advancement. Lacking that commitment, little economic change is likely to occur. Economic reforms to promote development generally must be accompanied by political reforms that mobilize government and societal institutions to make economic development and poverty reduction the primary goals. Reforms cannot come from outside— the commitment must come from within the country and its leadership, who must "own" the reforms. When reforms are successful they lead to a virtuous circle of economic growth and development. Countries make more efficient use of scarce resources and more external resources become available as foreign investors provide capital and foreign customers buy more of the country's output of goods and services.

The key role played by political leadership emphasizes the extent to which development is mainly a local phenomenon that depends highly on a country's conditions, culture, history, and policy decisions. Each country has its own social, political, and economic history. Thus, the path to development will be different in each case. As the 2002 Development Report of the World Bank puts it, "where countries are today affects where they can go."[22] The best overall approach is a pragmatic one, but with specific goals and principles, that focuses on taking advantage of opportunities that present themselves.

As a U.S.-based organization of business and academic leaders, we recognize the limits of our ability to influence the leaderships of developing countries. For the most part, the path toward economic success is already well marked for them, and the rewards for their nations are reasonably well known. What is missing in most cases is the political will to implement needed reforms. CED urges developing country governments to make economic growth and poverty reduction their primary priorities and to begin immediately to take the necessary steps to achieve those goals.

LOCAL PROBLEMS NEED LOCAL SOLUTIONS

The commitment and dedication of the local government leadership are necessary ingredients for economic development to take hold. Such commitments carry risks. Government programs to promote development can generate winners and losers, and can be destabilizing for the government that launches it. In some cases, dictators, military governments, or kleptocrats pursue goals at odds with the welfare of the general population. In other cases, vested political, economic, and social interests oppose changes that can undermine the bases of their power.

Government institutions play many roles, and improving the functions of government—good governance—is a key area of reform.[†] No simple solution exists to the

---

† "Good governance is epitomized by predictable, open and enlightened policy making; a bureaucracy imbued with professional ethos; an executive arm of government accountable for its actions; a strong civil society participating in public affairs; and all behaving under the rule of law." World Bank, World Development Report 2002.

problem of ineffectual governance or lack of leadership. Solutions must come from inside the country; outsiders cannot impose them, although conditionality and incentives from foreign government, investors, and civil groups may influence local choices. Good local solutions are likely to be enhanced by strong democratic processes. Democratic and participatory institutions help to keep governments focused on meeting the economic needs of the electorate and create an environment of accountability and openness to change. The existence of political and civil rights cause governments to pay greater attention to economic needs. It is a remarkable finding, for example, that famine has never occurred in a functioning democracy.[23]

Although economic development has occurred under authoritarian rule, little evidence exists that authoritarian policies promote economic growth. The right to express one's political preferences through elections is closely related to basic economic rights, just as the right to private property and to engage freely in trade and investment are inextricably linked to basic personal freedoms. Thus, economic rights generally are more consistent with a political system based on personal liberty and responsibility and the diffusion of power than one based on authoritarian rule.[24]

The key to economic growth is the creation of market-friendly policies. The rights to hold private property and to enforce private contracts form the foundation for mobilizing economic resources. Where private property rights are secure, property owners have a much greater incentive to use their property productively and efficiently and to undertake improvements to enhance its value.

A key issue facing some governments is how to establish formal title to property that already exists in the informal sector. The establishment of formal property rights, holding a clear title to one's land, home, or tools, may allow the property to be used as collateral for a loan.[25] However, formal ownership of

assets solves only a part of the problem. Governments must also ensure that market failures in the provision of finance to small property holders are corrected and that the overall financial system operates in a safe and sound manner. Developing micro-finance institutions that lend to small business that might not otherwise qualify for credit could be one method for helping small property holders. Many micro-finance institutions, such as *MicroStart* in Madagascar and *Pro Mujer* in Latin America, are particularly effective at helping women entrepreneurs.[26]

Another critical step is creating an independent judicial system that can adjudicate disputes and ensure the rights to use and dispose of property. More broadly, a legal and judicial system that is respected by the society as a source of justice is required for social stability. In either the broader social context or the specific role of adjudicating property disputes, the judiciary must have ethical integrity, independence from political interference, and impartiality. It should also be accessible and affordable to all classes.

The key impediment to reform is not so much the availability of resources, but the political will to implement change. Although the task is daunting, developing countries can find help among many public and private international groups. One significant venture is a public-private partnership between the American Bar Association and the United Nations Development Program. (See Box, The American Bar Association and the United Nations Development Program Partnership on Legal Resources)

TRANSPARENT GOVERNMENT AND THE ELIMINATION OF CORRUPTION

In many countries, a top priority in the establishment of a political foundation for economic growth is to root out corruption. Doing so would remove a significant burden

THE AMERICAN BAR ASSOCIATION AND THE UNITED NATIONS DEVELOPMENT PROGRAM PARTNERSHIP ON LEGAL RESOURCES

The American Bar Association (ABA) and the United Nations Development Program (UNDP) entered into a Project Cooperation Agreement in October 1999 to establish a Legal Resource Unit (LRU) within the ABA Section of International Law and Practice. The mission of the LRU is to provide a legal resource capability to service UNDP global governance programs and projects supporting legal reform and democratic institution building. The primary task of the LRU is to assist UNDP Country Offices to identify candidates capable of providing legal advice, normally on a pro bono basis, on the drafting of legislation, judicial reform, building of legal institutions including professional groups and associations, and other legal dimensions of governance. The functions of the LRU reflect UNDP program needs and include identification and selection of legal experts to work as resident and non-resident advisors, legal commentators, and legal facilitators.

AREAS OF WORK

LRU legal experts support UNDP program countries in a wide array of substantive legal areas. Including:

- Reform of legal institutions and systems, including reform of constitutional frameworks
- Support to electoral bodies and drafting of electoral laws
- Improvement of legislative drafting and parliamentary practices
- Reform of public-sector regulations and processes
- Strengthening anti-corruption measures
- Support for decentralization and strengthening of local institutions
- Development of the capacity of independent lawyers associations
- Legal education and judicial training
- Legal services to the indigent and underrepresented
- Other law-related areas as needed.

SOURCE: American Bar Association <www.abanet.org/intlaw/lru/>.

on domestic commerce, encourage open competition, and help to attract foreign investment and trade. As we have on previous occasions, CED continues to emphasize the critical importance of rooting out bribery and other forms of corruption.[27]

CED encourages developing country governments to make a clear and convincing commitment to ending bribery and corruption. They should eliminate types of regulation that reduce competition and serve as a breeding ground for bribery. They should operate in the open and be subject to scrutiny by civil society groups, which should monitor and report on bribery, corruption, and other abuses.

Government corruption imposes large economic costs and is associated with lower economic growth and per capita income.[28] Corruption can be viewed as a tax on certain economic transactions, a barrier to competition, and a subversion of the legitimacy of political institutions. Contrary to perceptions, corruption is a greater problem and generates greater costs for domestic businesses and households than it does for international firms. It exacts a substantial toll on the poor by denying them regular access to vital basic services. One report estimated that the average Mexican household spends up to 14 per cent of its income every year on bribing civil servants, police officers, and other public officials for such transactions as obtaining a driving license, obtaining a telephone, and enrolling a child in school.[29] Domestic firms are more numerous and have fewer choices than foreign ones, and the opportunities for victimization by corrupt officials are greater. Many multinational firms refuse to pay bribes to local officials. It has been illegal for U.S. firms to pay such bribes since the passage of the Foreign Corrupt Practices Act of 1977.

To counter corruption, governments need to establish institutions and incentives that both lower the potential for arbitrary and discretionary actions of public officials and raise the costs of engaging in corrupt practices. Basing necessary government interventions on market mechanisms rather than on bureaucratic controls reduces opportunities for corruption and is more economically efficient. For example, a tariff that affects the price of a good is preferable to a quota that imposes a quantity restriction, which may open the door for bribery

Democratic institutions such as regular independent elections, a free press, and a vibrant civil society have been shown to help reduce corruption. One organization that has been working in many countries and international institutions to shine a light on, and root out, corruption is Transparency International (TI). TI has been at the forefront of efforts to create both international conventions and national systems to support anti-corruption and good governance efforts. (See Box, Transparency International)

In 1999 the OECD *Convention on Combating Bribery of Foreign Public Officials in International Business Transactions* entered into force. The purpose of the convention was to address the supply side of corruption, which

is fed by corporations based in developed countries. It requires countries to make it a domestic criminal offense to bribe a foreign public official. To rectify a previous practice that supported bribery, countries are also required to deny the tax deductibility of such bribes. All 29 OECD members and 5 non-members (Argentina, Brazil, Bulgaria, Chile, and Slovakia) have ratified the convention.[30]

The OECD also has provided guidance to businesses by revising their *Guidelines for Multinational Enterprises* to include recommended measures to prevent both the furnishing and solicitation of bribes. The Guidelines also call for corporations to disclose political contributions and not to make illegal contributions to candidates for public office, political parties, and other political organizations. The OECD *Principles of Corporate Governance* were also revised to improve disclosure and transparency in financial reporting in ways that help discourage bribery.

Some corporations have established their own anti-corruption policies, including codes of ethical conduct that express the company's commitment not to engage in or condone bribery. Such internal codes establish a corporate culture that condemns corrupt behavior and establishes a commitment to the international anti-bribery conventions. In addition, companies create management and audit systems to monitor and review compliance annually. This is particularly true for joint ventures in which a global enterprise may own only a minority share of the equity.

An additional step that some global companies have taken to promote transparency is to expand the scope of reporting to include periodic public reports on their local activities. Although not directly linked to anti-corruption efforts, such transparent reporting sets an example for local companies to follow and establishes an atmosphere of openness. A leading example is the Global Reporting Initiative (GRI), which has established a

TRANSPARENCY INTERNATIONAL[a]

Transparency International (TI) is a non-governmental organization dedicated to curbing corruption and increasing government accountability. TI, with its administrative head office in Berlin, Germany, has national chapters in 80 countries, including the United States. TI forges coalitions between public authorities, governments, and civil society to support constructive initiatives to reduce opportunities for the acceptance and payment of bribes.

TRANSPARENCY INTERNATIONAL WORLD WIDE PROGRAM

TI major worldwide program activities include:

Capacity Building in Developing Counties

TI works to support the development and growth of civil society organizations in developing countries to build support for greater transparency in government and to monitor enforcement of anti-corruption regulations and laws.

Stimulating International Support for Anti-Corruption in Developing Countries

TI works closely with bilateral and multilateral development assistance agencies to strengthen the focus and content of anti-corruption aspects of aid projects and programs.

Developing Anti-Corruption Knowledge Management

TI, through its *Anti-Corruption Source Book, Global Corruption Report, Corruption Perception Index* and *Bribe Payers' Index,* and other publications, strengthens global knowledge of the full range of public policy and business issues related to corruption.

Promoting Anti-Corruption Conventions

TI has been the leading non-profit global organization campaigning in recent years for an OECD *Anti-Bribery Convention* and for similarly major incentives to criminalize the payment of bribes to foreign officials in a range of other international organizations.

Working with Business to Curb Global Corruption

TI works closely with major corporations through a series of special initiatives to strengthen anti-corruption work on a global basis. In this context, for example, TI is working with a number of defense companies on the issue of corruption in the international arms trade; TI is working with 11 major financial institutions on corruption and anti-money laundering; TI is working with a range of multinational corporations to define anti-corruption business principles.

TI-USA PROGRAM

The U.S. national chapter of TI is highly active in many of TI's special issues; it works with official agencies and the business community. In addition, TI-USA, on behalf of the global TI movement, plays leading fundraising roles and enjoys strong support from numerous U.S. corporations, U.S. foundations, and the U.S. Agency for International Development (USAID).

Procurement Reform

TI-USA has worked with the U.S. Administration, the private sector, and other TI chapters to promote the conclusion of a WTO *Agreement on Transparency in Government Procurement* and similar agreements in the FTAA and APEC. It promotes strong transparency provisions in U.S. bilateral trade agreements and a requirement that all bidders on World Bank and regional bank financed projects have anti-bribery programs.

Corporate Compliance

TI-USA participated in the International Chamber of Commerce committee that drafted the revised Rules of Conduct to Combat Extortion and Bribery and contributed to *Fighting Bribery, A Corporate Practices Manual.* It is participating in efforts to strengthen anti-bribery compliance programs and developing best practices for small and medium-size enterprises.

a. The following is based on information obtained at the Transparency International websites, <www.transparency.org/index.html> and <www.transparency-usa.org>.

generally accepted framework for voluntary reporting of the economic, environmental, and social performance of an organization.[31] GRI's goal is to make such reporting as routine and credible as financial reporting in terms of comparability, rigor, and verifiability. These reporting standards are supported by an increasing number of U.S.-based global corporations, such as AT&T, Ford, General Motors, Nike, and Procter & Gamble.

All countries should ratify the OECD *Anti-Bribery Convention* and fully prosecute under national laws the illegal payment of bribes. CED urges multinational corporations to abide by internationally recognized standards of integrity and consider implementing voluntary reporting practices that make public the impact of their activities on the domestic economy. They should also comply with relevant OECD conventions and other appropriate international codes against bribery and corruption.

Chapter 4

THE NEED FOR SOUND ECONOMIC POLICIES

Sound macro- and microeconomic policies are fundamental to achieving economic development goals, including the reduction of poverty. Although no one set of prescriptions fits all countries under all circumstances, the goals of economic policy remain clear and bear constant repetition. A substantial economic literature shows that countries with disciplined monetary and fiscal policy, extensive market-based competition, and openness to international trade and direct investment enjoy better long-run growth performance than countries without such policies.

APPROPRIATE MACROECONOMIC AND MICROECONOMIC POLICIES

Macroeconomic policies—fiscal, monetary, and exchange rate policies—do not conform to a single rule. Appropriate policies are dependent upon specific conditions. Nevertheless, most economists subscribe to the broad dictums that fiscal policy should be "disciplined," meaning that governments should live within their means, and monetary policy should aim to keep the general price level stable. International financial market integration should also be a goal for most developing countries since external capital is an important resource for economic growth. Therefore, an appropriate exchange rate policy must also be part of the equation. An economy can only pursue two out of three key policy goals simultaneously: an independent monetary policy, financial market integration with the rest of the world, and exchange rate

stability. As a result, exchange rate flexibility, which allows a country to have some monetary independence and an open financial market, has become an important practice in the wake of the Asian financial crisis. Although some small economies have successfully adopted a hard, pegged exchange rate, the crisis in Argentina has dramatically underscored the potential costs.

In general, the goal of microeconomic policies is to allow scarce resources to flow to their most valuable uses. The importance of using market competition to improve resource allocation cannot be overstated. Developing countries lack resources. Given such scarcity, resources need to be stretched as far as they can go. Experience has shown that relatively unfettered competitive markets provide the strongest foundation for efficient resource allocation, economic growth, and the alleviation of poverty. Competition gives powerful incentives for producers to supply the highest value for the lowest cost. It also acts as an engine for change and innovation. Through competition, firms are encouraged to raise productivity, which is the basis for higher incomes. In market-oriented economies, vigorous competition has produced a significant improvement in living standards, including those of the very poor. Opening the domestic economy to foreign trade and investment is one of the most powerful steps a government can take to promote competition. As discussed on the next page, international trade and foreign direct investment introduce lower cost goods and more efficient production methods.

Not all activities, of course, should or can be left to private markets. Governments must be able to levy taxes, correct market failures, and provide necessary public goods, such as national security, public health, education, and a clean environment. Governments also may wish to establish and enforce domestic laws in areas such as labor and environmental policy, as many already have done. However, governments need to evaluate carefully the consequences of their economic interventions to ensure that scarce resources are not wasted and that policies are likely to achieve their goals.

Economic regulation of specific industries or sectors of the economy should be avoided, except where need has been clearly demonstrated, as in the provision of financial services where experience has shown that regulation is essential to safeguard the functioning of the entire economy. Government subsidies and taxes distort prices and thereby give incorrect information to market participants about the true value and scarcity of resources. Complex regulation through licensing and other procedures creates extra cost for firms and provides greater scope for corruption. Those costs not only raise prices but also create barriers to market entry that create monopoly power. Cutting regulatory costs would be one way to encourage greater competition from domestic firms. Another important reform measure would be to establish a policy, similar to U.S. anti-trust policy, to prevent anti-competitive practices and outlaw abusive collusion by homegrown or international cartel members.

THE BENEFITS OF OPEN MARKETS FOR TRADE AND INVESTMENT

Developing economies that are more open to foreign trade and investment grow faster than closed economies. Faster economic growth raises incomes and reduces poverty.

International Trade

Early in 2001, CED published a policy statement, *From Protest to Progress: Addressing Labor and Environmental Conditions Through Freer Trade*, that made the case for freer trade. The reduction of trade barriers around the world has helped developing countries to increase economic growth and reduce poverty. Trade allows for greater specialization in production, which improves efficiency and makes possible higher incomes. Trade also brings fresh competition into domestic markets, thereby encouraging further efficiencies through innovation and capital investment. For small economies, trade provides a means to expand markets and gain economies of scale. Empirical research in the past decade has shown a positive and strong association over very long periods between openness to trade and economic growth.[32]

Developing countries have much to gain from lowering barriers to imports. Except in rare cases, for example when there are very large economies of scale, the protection of domestic industries serves only to raise the costs of goods and services and distort the allocation of domestic resources.* Governments of developed countries can help substantially by lowering barriers to developing country exports. Recommendations that address this point are discussed below.

Foreign Direct Investment

Foreign direct investment (FDI) is perhaps the most important and effective source of economic growth other than domestic saving. A recent study showed that, independent of domestic savings, a ten-percentage point rise in the ratio of FDI to GNP in developing countries raises the long-run steady-state income level by 3 percent.[33] We encourage developing country governments to make it one of their highest development priorities to attract foreign direct investment by pursuing sound economic policies and establishing a

---

*See memorandum by ALAN BELZER (page 60).

25

receptive climate for such investment. Governments should focus on establishing the preconditions for the successful attraction and use of FDI: the liberalization of restrictions on foreign ownership, a supportive and consistent macroeconomic policy and institutional framework, and the development of an educated and productive workforce.

With over 800,000 foreign affiliates worldwide, foreign direct investment is a key source of resource and technology transfer from the economically advanced countries. FDI also tends to have significant spillover benefits in the form of increased net exports, employment, and productivity. FDI increases competition in local product and labor markets, which puts pressure on domestic firms to improve efficiency. In contrast to other forms of capital inflows, FDI tends to be more stable because it is committed for a longer duration.

The most obvious way that foreign direct investment helps developing countries is through the transfer of capital. Foreign equity capital is a significant and stable source of external resources for developing countries. As indicated by Table 5, private direct investment is the only stable and growing source of net long-term resource flows to developing countries. FDI has remained relatively stable since 1997, after growing significantly since the beginning of the decade. The annual net

flow of FDI to developing countries, which was roughly equal to net official flows in 1992-1993 and prior years, rose to 4 times the level of net official flows in 1996-2000.[34] Total private flows, including debt and equity financing, accounted for over 86 percent of long-term resource flows to developing countries.

Some observers have argued that the scope for FDI to help most developing countries is limited because it is concentrated in just a few developing countries. In 2000, ten countries accounted for nearly three-quarters of all FDI in developing countries.[35] The reality, however, is more complex. FDI inflows were much more evenly distributed when measured against countries' gross fixed capital formation.[36] By that measure, for example, China (which ranks highest in total FDI) was only slightly above the average of 12.5 percent of gross fixed capital formation. FDI in Latin America and the Caribbean region was over 20 percent of gross fixed capital formation, and for the least developed countries of the Pacific it was nearly 30 percent.

The transfer of modern technology and business methods is another direct benefit that a country gains when a foreign company chooses to establish or expand an investment. The investment a company makes when it establishes a long-term equity position includes the transfer of technology, manage-

Table 5

Net Long-Term Resource Flows to Developing Countries
(billions of dollars)

	1991	1992	1993	1994	1995	1996	1997	1998	1999	2000	Avg (1991-1995)	% of Total	Avg (1996-2000)	% of Total
Total	123.0	155.8	220.4	223.7	261.2	311.2	342.6	334.9	264.5	295.8	196.8	100.0	309.8	100.0
Official flows	60.9	56.5	53.6	48.0	55.1	31.9	42.8	54.6	45.3	38.6	54.8	27.9	42.6	13.8
Private flows	62.1	99.3	166.8	175.7	206.1	279.3	299.8	280.3	219.2	257.2	142.0	72.1	267.2	86.2
of which:														
Capital markets	26.3	52.2	100.2	85.6	99.1	147.8	127.2	103.5	33.8	79.2	72.7	36.9	98.3	31.7
Foreign Dir. Inv.	35.7	47.1	66.6	90.0	107.0	131.5	172.6	176.8	185.4	178.0	69.3	35.2	168.9	54.5

SOURCE: World Bank, *Global Development Finance*, 2001.

ment expertise, and other skills and intangibles, such as a global brand name, supply chain, and distribution network. Such investment also creates trade linkages, both within and outside the recipient country through intra-corporate transactions and other channels. Internal linkages to suppliers, customers, and even competitors can generate especially significant economic benefits. Most productive enterprises buy a large proportion of inputs locally. A foreign affiliate that buys local inputs adds to domestic demand and encourages more specialized and efficient production. They may also provide domestic suppliers with access to improved technology or business methods. Unrelated firms and competitors may adopt these new methods or gain from access to more highly knowledgeable and skilled workers.

In labor markets, affiliates of multinational firms operating in developing countries often pay higher wages and provide more extensive fringe benefits than their domestic counterparts. While not all foreign investors pay more and do more for their employees, many provide employment benefits, such as health care and educational services that are not required by domestic law. They also may improve local worker skills with advanced training methods that are often not available in local schools. Where foreign employers provide such benefits, they help raise standards in the domestic employment market.

Several factors appear important in attracting FDI. One is the combination of good governance and good economic policies. Foreign investors are generally unwilling to commit resources to countries with unstable governments and unsound economic policies. The existence or history of economic, social, or political instability, while not an absolute bar, is a substantial discouragement to foreign investors who have global opportunities. Moreover, experience has shown that countries with inconsistent macroeconomic policies, weak financial supervision, and substan-

tial microeconomic distortions are unprepared to benefit from foreign capital inflows. Another, discussed in more detail below, is education. Most FDI from advanced economies to developing countries has gone to countries with at least a minimum stock of human capital needed to absorb the transfer of technology. Research suggests that FDI contributes relatively more to economic growth than does domestic investment in situations where an educated labor force exists.[37]

In general, developing country governments are very aware of the steps they must take to attract foreign capital, even if they do not act on that knowledge. Reports by private firms, such as the Frank Russell Company's *EMPulse Reports* on investor perceptions and other similar investor-oriented indices, bond rating agencies, and the World Bank Group regularly evaluate the investment climate in developing countries. Respondents to a business environment survey carried out by the World Bank emphasized the importance of good governance to decisions about conducting business in developing countries. Tax concessions and other incentives have very little attraction if the overall investment climate is unsound. At the top of the list of obstacles to doing business were taxes and regulations, inflation, political instability, corruption, and street crime.[38] Savvy foreign investors also note what local investors are doing with their money, since the locals know the investment landscape much better than the foreigners. If local capital is leaving the country, the message to potential foreign investors is quite clear.

Building on TRIMS to Create a Multilateral Investment Code

Trade and investment are often viewed as alternative ways for a business to enter foreign markets. However, changes in the nature of international business and the growth of transnational corporations has meant that trade and investment are often complements rather than substitutes. About one-third of all trade takes place among affiliates of international corporations. In the case of the United States, trade among units of the same global enterprise accounts for 50 percent of all U.S. merchandise trade. Of this intra-firm trade, 60 percent is within U.S.-based enterprises and 40 percent within foreign-based enterprises with corporate units in the United States.

The economic value of foreign direct investment and its relationship to trade is recognized to some degree by the World Trade Organization (WTO) *Agreement on Trade-Related Investment Measures* (TRIMs) and by the *General Agreement on Trade in Services* (GATS). Both agreements strive to extend the WTO principle of national treatment to the investment arena.[†] A shortcoming of both agreements, however, is that they are limited to only certain trade aspects of investment. TRIMs apply only to measures that affect trade in goods. It forbids making trade-distorting measures such as "local content" and "trade balancing" requirements for eligibility for investment incentives. Similarly, GATS is directed at ensuring national treatment only for foreign companies that need to set up operations within a country in order to supply certain services.

The United States should push to extend the WTO's *Agreement on Trade-Related Investment Measures* (TRIMs) into a more effective multilateral investment code. The primary goal of such a code should be to create a common set of rules for the national treatment of foreign direct investment. In addition, countries should agree to report publicly their use of special incentives to attract investment, such as tax abatements and other financial inducements, and submit them to review by the WTO. Such trans-parency could help rein in the use of such incentives by all WTO members and discourage policies that might reduce labor and environmental standards to attract foreign investment.

An aborted attempt to create an international investment code took place in negotiations under the auspices of the OECD for a *Multilateral Agreement on Investment* (MAI), starting in 1995. The MAI was an attempt to foster additional investment activity by liberalizing and standardizing the diverse bilateral investment treaties (known as BITs) that govern the treatment of foreign investment on a country-to-country basis. Unlike the WTO, which governs the flow of goods and services through multilateral commitments extended through "most-favored-nation" treatment, no international institution or agreement exists to encourage and monitor the global flow of direct investment, with the exception of provisions of TRIMs and GATS mentioned above.

The MAI was designed to assemble the elements of the various existing BITs into a systematic whole. The draft agreement was defined by three major elements. It would have required countries to treat foreign companies in the same way as local companies (national treatment), banned performance requirements, and established a process for effective dispute settlement procedures by providing access to binding international arbitration of disputes between investors and the state. By 1998, when a draft of the agreement was revealed, it foundered for lack of support among those, including many developing countries, who viewed the OECD as the wrong organization to promote such an agreement and who were suspicious of both the lack of transparency in reaching the proposed draft and the motives of the United States in promoting it.

The need for a multilateral investment agreement still exists. The final declaration of the WTO ministerial conference in Doha recognized "the case for a multilateral frame-

[†] National treatment means that no distinction is made between foreign and domestic firms in domestic law and commerce. All are treated the same.

work to secure transparent, stable and predictable conditions for long-term cross-border investment, particularly foreign direct investment."[39] However, negotiations were deferred until after the next ministerial conference.

The TRIMs and GATS agreements do not sufficiently establish investment rights for international firms; nor do they address, as they should, the potential for investment incentives to spur a "race to the bottom." Competition among developing countries for foreign investment can create a bidding war that leads the host country "winner" to give away more in incentives than it gains in employment and income. (Similar bidding wars exist between U.S. states vying to be the location of foreign automobile producers and other manufacturers.) In some cases, such winners have clearly overbid. In the case of a developing country, the potential benefits of luring a major foreign manufacturer may appear so large that the government will offer more lucrative incentives than it should. A requirement to disclose publicly the details of investment incentives would be an important tool to educate all countries about the costs of such incentives and could lead them to be more judicious in the use of incentives.

What the United States and Other Developed Countries Can Do

To the extent that developing country governments commit themselves to market-led economic growth, they will gain economic resources through foreign direct investment. The United States and other developed countries impose few barriers to investments abroad other than certain national security restrictions. Such investments are driven almost entirely by conditions in the receiving country and market factors, such as proximity to markets, relative costs, and expected returns. (See Box, FDI and the U.S. Economy)

Developing countries also gain resources by exporting goods and services to more

developed economies (as well as to other developing countries). Better access to markets in developed countries is especially important for developing countries that are committed to fostering market-based economic growth. **The United States and other developed countries should reduce trade barriers to developing country products and services. The United States should take the lead in the WTO to ensure that developing countries have access to developed country markets. It should seek to speed up the implementation of tariff reductions under the *Agreement on***

FDI AND THE U.S. ECONOMY[a]

Globalization critics argue that outward foreign direct investment from the United States hurts the U.S. economy, especially U.S. workers. The truth is quite the opposite. Outward investment by U.S.-based firms helps them perform better. American enterprises with ownership stakes in foreign production or other activities have higher worker productivity, use frontier technologies more intensively, and report higher growth in productivity than do similar U.S. firms that are not invested abroad. Workers in the United States employed at U.S-owned multinationals earn on average 18 percent more than at comparable-sized non-multinational firms.

Although individual cases exist which link a particular plant closing in the United States to a specific overseas investment, outward FDI is not a major cause of unemployment. Indeed, research indicates that at an industry level outward FDI creates more jobs than it destroys. Jobs created are most likely to be in higher-paying sectors and the jobs destroyed in lower-paying sectors.

a. Based on Howard Lewis III and J. David Richardson, *Why Global Commitment Really Matters*, IIE, 2001, and Linda Lim, *The Globalization Debate: Issues and Challenges*, ILO, 2001.

Textiles and Clothing (which replaced the *Multi-Fiber Arrangement*) and tighten WTO rules on anti-dumping so that only the most worthy complaints would qualify for protection. Production subsidies for domestic agriculture, which are especially heavy in the European Union and Japan, should also be eliminated.

As a result of low labor costs and other factors, developing countries tend to specialize in the production of labor-intensive goods—often simple manufactured items such as textiles and clothing—and agricultural products. Although average trade barriers in developed countries are relatively low, barriers to imports of agricultural products, textiles, and clothing are exceptionally high. (See Figure 1) Developed country governments, to protect their domestic industries from competition via lower-priced imports, have employed tariffs and quotas to lower the supply and increase the price of such imports. These trade barriers handicap the ability of developing countries to export agricultural and other labor-intensive products, which could provide additional employment and income for many of the world's poor. Trade in textiles and clothing accounts for nearly one-fifth of developing countries exports of manufactures.[40] Agricultural products, in the form of food products and agricultural raw materials, account for approximately 11 percent of all developing country exports.[41]

A World Bank simulation shows that incomes in developing countries could rise by an additional 5 percent by 2015 if all import tariffs, export subsidies, and domestic production subsidies were eliminated and phased-in starting in 2005.[42] The combined static and dynamic gains from more trade would provide an estimated $1.5 trillion of additional income in developing countries between 2005-2015. Developed countries would also benefit as they removed subsidies and import barriers, which distort their markets and reduce their incomes. They could gain as

Figure 1

Peak Tariff Levels by Product Group
(in percent, 1999)

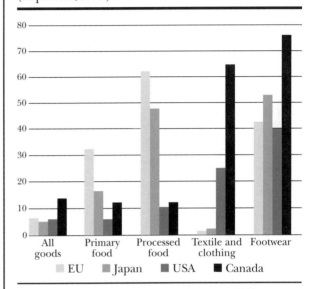

SOURCE: World Bank, *Global Economic Prospects*, 2002.

much as 1 percent of additional national income in 2015.

One of the negotiating goals, and accomplishments, of developing countries during the Uruguay rounds of trade negotiations was to gain improved market access for their principal exports. Two agreements, the *Agreement on Agriculture* and the *Agreement on Textiles and Clothing*, incorporated commitments from the developed country governments to reduce significantly barriers for agricultural, textile, and clothing products. Because the agreements included long phase-in periods and other limitations, progress in reducing barriers for developing country exports has been limited; high barriers still remain. Negotiations for market access in these areas is now high on the agenda of the new trade round launched in Doha.

Agriculture. The Uruguay Round *Agreement on Agriculture* (URAA) was an important, albeit incomplete, step towards the reduction of barriers to entry for agricultural goods into high-income economies. The major achievement of the agreement was the conversion of non-tariff restrictions, namely quotas, into tariffs. That conversion made trade restrictions more transparent and harder to increase. The agreement also established a schedule for tariff reductions, beginning in 1995.[†]

The trade barrier reductions have been less successful than anticipated. Barriers to agriculture products cost developing countries an estimated $20 billion in lost exports each year.[43] The average tariff imposed by industrialized countries on agricultural goods is still 14 percent, almost five times higher than the average tariff on industrial products.[≠]

Additional agricultural trade distortions include production and export subsidies. High-income nations spend over $300 billion annually to support domestic agricultural products.[44] That is about six times the level of all international development assistance. Such subsidies lead to over-production of agricultural products, which depresses world prices and forces developing country agricultural exports to compete at a disadvantage in world markets.

Textiles and Clothing. The Uruguay Round *Agreement on Textiles and Clothing* (ATC) promised the phase-out and eventual elimination of quotas on textiles and clothing. The ATC replaced the *Multi-Fiber Arrangement* (MFA), which had allowed developed countries to maintain quotas on imports from developing countries. The ATC established a four-stage integration plan. Sixteen percent of products would be brought under normal trade rules by January

1995, an additional 17 percent by January 1998, and 18 percent by January 2002. The remaining 49 percent would automatically be integrated at the end of the transitional period in 2005.

The effectiveness of the agreement in opening markets has been limited. Developed nations have been able to fulfill their legal commitments for the first three stages without reducing the most significant barriers. One reason for this is that half of the phase-out process was put off until 2005. In addition, the choice of products to be to be phased out was left to the importing countries and framed in terms of number of products rather than their value. Thus, although developed countries integrated one third of the *products* in the first two years as required, that only amounted to 6 percent in terms of *value.*[45]

Anti-Dumping Duties. For many years CED has advocated limits on the use of antidumping cases to protect domestic producers from foreign competition.[46] Both the WTO and U.S. trade law permit an importing country to apply anti-dumping duties when domestic producers suffer material injury as a result of imports entering the country at prices below those charged in home markets or below their estimated cost of production. U.S. law as applied to domestic trade, however, does not generally regard such price discrimination as unfair unless it can be shown to be predatory, that is, unless it is aimed at monopolization of the market. Such differences in treatment support the contention that U.S. antidumping law discriminates against imports.

Although the United States generally has fewer and less significant restrictions on trade than most other countries, it has been the heaviest user of antidumping law. It investigates more cases, imposes more and higher duties, and leaves those duties in place longer than other countries.[47] Consequently, many developing countries have established

---

† Developed countries agreed to reduce tariffs by an average of 36 percent over six years for all agricultural products. A minimum 15 percent reduction of tariffs on every product was also agreed to.

≠ One reason why restrictions remain high is that the agreement used a base period of 1986-1988 for the tariff conversions, when world commodity prices were exceptionally low.

similar antidumping laws to retaliate against U.S. practice, and developing country governments have made the limitation of antidumping cases one of their key negotiating objectives during the current round of trade negotiations. This is a good example of a policy where a "concession" on the part of the United States would lead to greater economic gains. Although some industries might lose protection through denial of anti-dumping duties, others would gain from access to lower-priced inputs. Consumers would clearly be better off.

Assisting Displaced Workers. Rather than inhibiting competition by protecting domestic firms and workers, we should enhance the ability of the economy to adjust to changed circumstances by enhancing job skills and retraining for workers. **In conjunction with reducing trade barriers and tightening standards for anti-dumping actions, the United States should bolster its system of adjustment assistance. As part of this effort, it should adopt a limited system of wage and health insurance for displaced workers.** CED has long recognized the need to provide adjustment assistance to workers displaced by trade, both as a matter of equity and to reduce the political barriers to liberalization.[48] Most recently, in a policy statement supporting the upcoming trade round, we reiterated our view that workers displaced from their jobs by layoffs, from all sources, should be eligible for assistance in adjusting to new circumstances.[49] Specifically, we support a program of temporary supplemental wage and health assistance for workers reemployed at less than their previous wage. Such a system, properly implemented, could a go long way to reduce worker anxiety about economic change, expand choice and benefit domestic consumers, make it easier to lower barriers to trade from developing countries, and allow the people of those countries to earn higher incomes.

Chapter 5

BEYOND OPEN MARKETS: INVESTING IN PEOPLE

Many developing country governments do not give adequate support to public education, public and private health care, and other basic social programs. In some cases neglect of these programs stems from a misunderstanding of their roles in economic development; in other cases it is simply due to a lack of resources. A common view has been that resources devoted to health and education could be better spent in support of more directly productive activities. A more comprehensive view of poverty that has emerged is that low income is often a consequence of a lack of education and adequate health.[50] Spending to overcome those deficits should be viewed as investments in productive human capital, and donors are increasingly resolved to ensure that funding is adequate to meet education and health needs.

Investments in primary education, health, and nutrition enhance the productive capacity of not only low-income individuals, but of the whole economy. Investments devoted to women's education and health are particularly important and intertwined. Literacy, for example, enables women to understand basic health information and to act accordingly, in the best interests of their children and families. Women also play a critical role as agents of change who promote social transformations needed for economic development.[51]

We encourage all relevant public and private organizations to contribute to the improvement of education and health outcomes in developing countries. Developing country governments should make it one of their top priorities to improve the delivery

and quality of education and health services. Similarly, developed country governments should focus attention and development assistance funding on improving education and health, especially in the poorest countries. In addition, we encourage multinational corporations, as employers, to provide appropriate education, training, and health services for their employees.

In each of these endeavors, special attention and resources should be dedicated to improving the status of women: investments in the education and health of women have high social rates of return because of their work and family roles. Similarly, development programs that assist small businesses, farmers, and other commercial ventures should recognize the unique contributions of women.

As detailed below, most governments are paying more attention to education and health through various global conferences, aid agencies, international organizations, and public-private partnerships. We are cognizant of these efforts; our goal is not to invent new programs or add new layers of complexity, but to support the positive efforts of existing programs. We caution, however, that for these programs to be successful the policy environments emphasized above — good governance, sound macroeconomic policies, and open markets — must also be in place.

An important effort is being taken in this direction through the Enhanced Heavily Indebted Poor Countries (HIPC) Initiative. This multilateral program, which was supported by CED at its inception, ties debt forgiveness for the poorest developing countries to a

comprehensive framework of poverty reduction through investments in education, health,
and other social programs within a sound fiscal framework.[52] By reducing or eliminating
debt payments, the program makes more
funds available for other purposes. However, it
is up to local officials to determine how those
funds are to be used. To participate in the
HIPC program, a country must implement an
IMF/World Bank-supported adjustment program during a six-year period. The most
promising aspect of the program for meeting
social policy goals and enhancing prospects
for development is the link between debt
relief and poverty reduction. Each government participating in the HIPC program is
required to develop a "Poverty Reduction
Strategy Paper" (PRSP) that indicates the

actions it intends to take to improve access to
health, education, the social safety net, and
for other purposes. (See Box, Poverty-
Reducing Spending in PRSP) The strategy,
developed with the assistance of the World
Bank and IMF, must ensure consistency
between a country's macroeconomic and
social policies.

Our support for the HIPC Initiative is
predicated on its effectiveness in shifting
resources towards the stated poverty reduction objectives. It appears that the IMF and
World Bank have taken appropriate steps to
establish expenditure tracking systems to
ensure that funds released by debt forgiveness
go towards the objectives defined in the
PRSPs. Because funds are fungible, tracking
systems must cover overall government spend-

POVERTY-REDUCING SPENDING IN PRSPS

PRSPs seek to shift the composition of public spending towards poverty-reducing
programs. The degree of elaboration and specificity of policies and targets to achieve
poverty-reduction goals varies across countries. Programs also vary in terms of the coverage,
magnitude, and speed. Some countries explicitly target yearly reductions in the incidence
of poverty. Intermediate targets often include goals for primary education (typically enrollment rates), basic health care (typically infant, child, and maternal mortality rates), and the
incidence of transmissible and endemic diseases, including HIV/AIDS, improvements in
social infrastructure, and in some countries, reduction in regional and gender disparities.

The main features of country strategies are as follows:

In general, most propose:

- enhancing access of the poor to primary education, with emphasis on reducing gender
  and regional disparities. The strategies also promote better quality and efficiency in
  the education sector

- enhancing access to primary and preventive health care services

- emphasizing infrastructure programs in the areas of water, roads, electricity, and
  telecommunications.

Some also propose:

- Providing housing to the poor

- Strengthening social safety nets to include food subsidies or other food security
  programs, social assistance programs, labor-intensive public works, and food for work
  programs.

SOURCE: International Monetary Fund and International Development Association, *Tracking of Poverty-Reducing Public Spending in Heavily Indebted Poor Countries (HIPCs)*, March 2001.

ing, not just those items targeted to receive HIPC-related funding. The ability to track funds relates directly to the ability of anti-poverty programs to achieve their objectives. More fundamentally, as pointed out by an IMF/World Bank review of the program, better tracking of public funding can improve the efficiency and effectiveness of all government programs. "The management and monitoring of public expenditures is not merely a technical challenge but also fundamentally a deeper governance challenge."[53]

The following analysis is meant to highlight some of the more important aspects of education, health, and social policies. It is not meant to be an exhaustive treatment. Rather, our purpose is to illustrate some of the many ways in which development programs can make sound economic investments that can both ameliorate the immediate consequences of poverty and attack some of its root causes.

EDUCATION FOR ALL

Attainment of basic literacy and numeracy skills is among the most significant factors in reducing poverty and increasing participation by individuals in the economic, political, and cultural life of their societies.[54] Higher levels of education and workforce training rely on these skills. Research by the World Bank shows that economic growth rates were especially high in countries with high levels of both education and macroeconomic stability and openness.[55]

International development goals call for universal primary education in all countries and the equal enrollments of boys and girls.[†]

In some countries both the overall and gender-specific enrollment gaps are very wide.

The Importance of Universal Access

Most experts view universal access to primary education as a prerequisite to lifting people from poverty. In the right setting, education promotes economic well-being and poverty reduction by increasing human capital. People with higher levels of education generally have better health, are more productive, and, therefore, have increased incomes. In the poorest nations, each additional year of schooling raises earning power by 10 to 20 percent.[56] Once basic education is more widely available, on-the-job training can provide higher-level skills. For societies as a whole, education has spillover benefits that affect public health, good governance, economic growth, and environmental protection.

Despite these findings, 113 million children around the world, or about 14 percent of all children, have never attended school. Another 150 million children drop out of school before completing five years. Approximately 97 percent of these children live in developing nations, and over one-third reside in sub-Saharan Africa. As a result, one out of every three children in developing countries does not attain five years of basic education.[57]

Many obstacles impede achieving education goals. Perhaps the largest obstacle in those countries with the lowest educational attainment is political commitment and leadership to make universal and gender-equal education a priority. Other factors that impede progress include the spread of HIV/AIDS and other infectious diseases, civil war and conflict, and rapid population growth.[†]

For other countries, the biggest hurdle is a lack of adequate funding. Many governments spend too little on education. They have high

---

† Education is considered a fundamental human right. In 1948, the Universal Declaration of Human Rights recognized the right to free and compulsory education as a fundamental right. The United Nations Convention on the Rights of Children reaffirmed this right in 1989. There are currently 191 countries that have ratified the convention, committing themselves to ensuring the right of every child to a basic education. The only two countries that have not are Somalia and the United States.

---

† A chronic lack of quality data on education makes both the attainment and assessment of goals particularly difficult.

student-to-teacher ratios, poorly trained teachers, and inadequate facilities. But they also have severe budgetary constraints and must live within their means if they are to achieve macroeconomic goals. While developing countries provide 98 percent of their own education funding, the 2 percent from external sources can be critical.[58] Despite pledges by developed countries to provide adequate funding to all countries with a viable national action plan for education, international support has been uneven and inadequate. Overall annual education support from OECD countries is approximately $3.5 billion. Support for basic education is about $700 million, representing about 1.2 percent of total bilateral official development aid.[59] The HIPC initiative is expected to make available an additional $600-700 million annually for education spending. Estimates of the need for external financing to reach agreed-upon goals put the cost at roughly $12 billion per year.[†60]

The Importance of Gender Equality

Educating females has been identified as having a particularly high rate of return and a high correlation with improvements in public health and the slowing of population growth. Cross-country studies suggest that if the Middle East and North Africa, South Asia, and Sub-Saharan Africa had been as successful as East Asia in narrowing the gender gap in education during 1960-1990, GNP per capita in those regions would have grown substantially faster.[61]

Two objectives motivate the targeting of gender equality for females in educational programs. The first is to ensure that women are given the same opportunities as men. The second, and perhaps more important from a development perspective, is that the educa-

tion of girls and women has widespread benefits and a high rate of return in terms of social improvements. In the most direct way, the education of women gives them an ability to find employment outside the home and earn an independent income. That empowerment can in turn lead to far reaching changes in traditional societies, not the least of which is to improve the health, life expectancy, and welfare of women themselves. Women's education is also strongly correlated with improvements in public health especially for children and with reductions in fertility rates, which lowers population growth. World Bank studies show that countries that invest in the education of girls have higher rates of economic growth. Specific benefits exist in rural areas, where educated women have been shown to more readily adopt new technologies and take greater advantage of agricultural extension and credit programs to raise productivity.

The Education for All Initiative

Global efforts to promote universal education have been supported by the Education for All (EFA) initiative, a program that originated at the *World Conference on Education for All* in Jomtien, Thailand in 1990 and was reaffirmed at the World Education Forum in Dakar, Senegal in 2000. At the Jomtien conference, representatives from 155 countries established a plan to make primary education universal and to increase literacy. The plan identified several goals, including improving access to early childhood care and development programs, increasing adult literacy, eliminating gender disparities in education, and providing universal access to primary education. The delegates pledged to achieve these goals by the year 2000.

By 2000 progress had been mixed at best, with wide variation from region to region. High-income countries' enrollment rates are near 100 percent, and Latin America and East Asia both appear to be on track to achieve

---

† Due to differences in methodologies and population, enrollment, and expenditure statistics, estimations range between $8 billion and $15 billion in additional education spending. $15 billion (UNESCO/UIS), $13 billion (World Bank), $9 billion (UNICEF), $8 billion (Oxfam).

universal access to primary education in the near future. In South Asia and sub-Saharan Africa, however, enrollment rates still range below 75 percent, with four of every ten sub-Saharan African children never attending school. (See Figure 2)

Globally, the number of enrolled children increased between 1990 and 2000 from 600 million to 680 million, which raised the total enrollment rate from 80 to 84 percent. The number of children without access to school was reduced from 127 million to 113 million in the same period. According to the World Bank, 76 developing countries have either already achieved universal primary education or are on pace to do so by 2015, 27 countries have made progress but may not reach the target, and 32 are unlikely to meet the EFA goal.[62] In many countries, education systems have been unable to keep pace with population growth. Thus, for example, although enrollment rates in sub-Saharan Africa have

increased from 54 percent to 60 percent, the absolute number of primary-school-aged children without access to school has actually increased. Population growth in sub-Saharan Africa is expected to increase the school-age population by over 34 million in the next 15 years.[63] The goal for gender equality also remains unfulfilled. Nearly 60 percent of unschooled children are girls.

The EFA initiative was renewed in 2000 in the Dakar Framework for Action. The Dakar framework commits governments to achieve quality basic education for all by 2015 or earlier, with particular emphasis placed on girls' education. It declares that individual governments are ultimately responsible for implementing the EFA through country-specific national action plans that set out budget and policy priorities, and calls on developed nations, non-governmental organizations, and development agencies to provide, among other things, technical and financial support.

Figure 2

Primary-School-Aged Children in Developing Countries, by Region

(in millions)

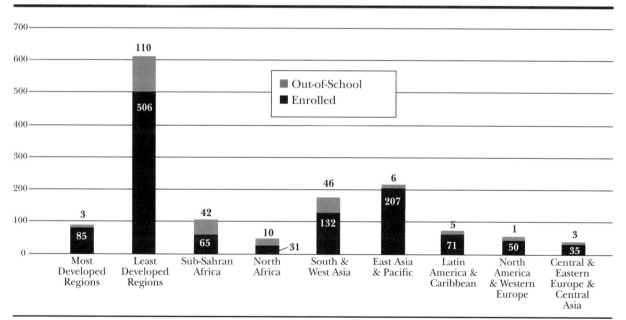

SOURCE: UNESCO, *Education for All 2000 Assessment*, Executive Summary.

It includes a pledge that "no countries seriously committed to basic education for all will be thwarted in their achievement of this goal by a lack of resources."[64]

The framework establishes strategies for the achievement of education goals and sets three major deadlines:

- 2002 – Finalization of national plans of action with concrete strategies for achieving the Dakar goals.

- 2005 – Achievement of equality for boys and girls in access to primary and secondary education.

- 2015 – Achievement of Education for All-deadline for universal primary education and a 50 percent improvement in levels of adult literacy.

The Dakar meeting assigned to the United Nations Educational, Scientific, and Cultural Organization (UNESCO) the responsibility for coordinating global EFA efforts. This effort complements those of national governments by coordinating and mobilizing participants, including multilateral and bilateral funding agencies, non-governmental organizations, and the private sector. Thus far, UNESCO has established an annual high-level meeting to sustain political momentum, created working groups to provide technical assistance for country and regional EFA programs, and established an EFA Observatory to monitor progress towards the successful completion of EFA.

Distance Learning

In a report released in 2001, CED suggested that developing countries could make greater use of Internet technologies to further their economic development efforts, and in particular to address literacy issues.[65] By utilizing modern technologies, distance learning allows people to transcend physical distance barriers and gain access to education sources.

In developing countries, where nations struggle to find the resources necessary to fund education systems, distance learning provides a potentially low-cost avenue for students and workers to gain access to knowledge and training.

Recent innovation in communications technology has helped in the emergence of distance learning. Although the concept is not new—educators have used television and radio as communications mediums for decades—the expansion of the Internet has greatly enhanced its applicability. Efforts to improve developing countries access to the Internet, like those of the G-8 Digital Opportunity Task (DOT) Force, will further enhance the effectiveness of distance learning methods.

Increasingly, investing in distance learning is seen as a way to educate more people without significant additional expenditures on local education infrastructure. It has emerged as a potential means for developing countries to meet increases in school enrollments. Although distance learning has been used mostly in higher education settings, it appears to be adaptable to primary education and could be used more both as an educational tool and as a means to bridge the so-called digital divide.

HEALTH

Poverty and health are interrelated as causes and consequences. Workers in poor health have low productivity and, hence, low income. People with low income typically lack the resources to maintain good health and diet.

Improvements in health result in increases in lifespan, productivity, income, and a society's prospects for economic growth. Improvements in the health of the poorest through immunizations and environmental enhancements typically have very high social rates of return, in part because they improve economic and health outcomes for everyone.[66]

The health of the world's poorest people could be greatly improved by targeting a relatively small set of diseases and conditions. Of greatest impact would be the control of communicable diseases, such as HIV/AIDS, malaria, and tuberculosis, and the improvement of maternal and child health. Together, AIDS, malaria, and tuberculosis (TB) cause 10 percent of all deaths worldwide, 35 percent of deaths in Africa.[67]

According to the World Bank, each year about two million childhood deaths occur due to diseases that can be prevented by vaccine, 7.5 million children die during early life, and 30 percent of the world is still without access to safe drinking water and sanitation systems.[68] At the same time, as a result of new knowledge about the causes, prevention, and treatment of diseases, the introduction of new policies that improve the effectiveness of health systems, and physical improvements in housing, sanitation, and water supplies, health outcomes in many developing countries are better overall than they have ever

been. However, where AIDS has taken its deadly toll, countries have experienced a reversal from previous gains. (See Figure 3)

A report released at the end of 2001 by the World Health Organization's Commission on Macroeconomics and Health (CMH) examined the relationships between health and economic outcomes in developing countries.[69] The Commission concluded that health is a necessary factor for facilitating economic growth, and recommended allocating increased funds to the health sector by developing country and donor country governments alike. The CMH predicted that eight million lives could be saved annually by increasing funding for health services. Conversely, without additional funding for health services, the spread of disease and the high number of preventable deaths will continue to slow economic growth in developing countries. New technologies are not needed to achieve these gains against mortality. Existing technologies and known health interventions have the widest application in saving

Figure 3

Changes in Life Expectancy in Countries with High HIV/AIDS Prevalence
(in millions)

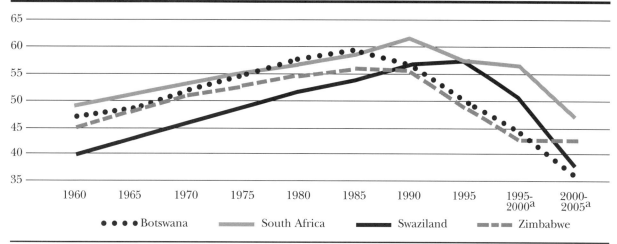

a. Estimates

SOURCES: World Bank, *World Development Indicators Database*, and United Nations Population Division, *World Population Prospects*, 2000 Revision.

lives—the challenge is putting the right tools and incentives in place.

As with most issues in developing countries, significant differences exist from country to country. Problems faced by the poorest countries command the most urgent attention. In particular, the problems of sub-Saharan Africa, where disease presents a significant barrier to economic growth, must be addressed as part of a comprehensive development strategy.[70] In general, health programs in low-income developing countries should stress improving the effectiveness of national public health systems. In addition, public health strategies should include a broad array of programs, such as education, pest control, improved sanitation, and roads that can make urbanized and better-served areas more accessible to rural patients.

Public Health, Women's Health, the HIV/AIDS Epidemic, and the Role of Global Businesses

The subject of health in developing countries is broad and cannot be treated comprehensively in this report. Below, we consider three high-priority subjects and examine how efforts to improve health outcomes relate to each. We also examine the role that global businesses can play in improving health outcomes.

Public Health

Control of communicable diseases and improved maternal and child health is at the top of public health priorities in the poorest countries. "The main causes of avoidable deaths in the low-income countries are HIV/AIDS, malaria, tuberculosis (TB), childhood infectious diseases, maternal and perinatal conditions, micronutrient deficiencies, and tobacco-related illnesses."[71] For middle-income countries that have already reduced mortality from communicable diseases, non-communicable diseases tend to be the highest priority. These include cardiovascular disease, diabetes, mental illnesses, and cancers, many of which can be effectively addressed by relatively low-cost interventions.

A broad consensus exists that investments in public health, through low-level facilities that emphasize preventative and simple curative activities, would have very high rates of return. In particular, the reallocation of public budgets toward support of preventative primary health care, nutrition, and sanitation programs are estimated to be more effective than many current programs aimed at treatment. According to the CMH, a "close-to-client" system would require few hospitals and could be delivered at health centers, smaller health outposts, and outreach services. Recent global initiatives for control of such diseases as TB, leprosy, and guinea-worm, provide useful models for such a system. Importantly, these initiatives included rigorous systems of monitoring, evaluation, reporting, and financial control, to ensure that resources were fully accountable.[72]

Creating public health, nutrition, and sanitation systems to match this consensus is lagging. Resource constraints are an obvious problem, but some health interventions can be delivered at relatively low cost, especially since labor costs are relatively low in most developing countries. Development aid agencies such as the World Bank are trying to ensure that sufficient resources are dedicated to effective health and nutrition programs. A portion of HIPC resources is to be spent in support of health programs.

The CMH recommendation is that, on average, low-and middle-income countries should increase budgetary outlays for health by 1 percent of GNP by 2007 and 2 percent by 2015. (See Table 6) They recommend that developed countries also commit additional resources to ensure that a lack of funds does not limit any country's capacity to provide health services. All donor funding should be conditioned on a strong and sustained commitment on the part of domestic governments to implement health reforms.

To ensure that additional resources could be effectively absorbed, health-based aid would be phased-in. Currently, total health-based aid stands at approximately $7 billion. By 2007, total assistance under the CMH recommendation would be increased to $27 billion, with $20 billion devoted to assistance for low-income countries in developing health systems, $3 billion to research devoted to the diseases of the poor, and $2 billion to the increased delivery of global public goods through international agencies. By 2015, total assistance would rise to $38 billion.

The CMH vision of a close-to-client system would involve a mix of state and non-state health service providers, the funding of which would be publicly guaranteed. In some poor countries, the public health system is so weak that a considerable non-governmental health sector has developed based on private practice, religiously affiliated providers, and private non-profit organizations. Research suggests that having a variety of providers provides competition and raises the quality of public health programs.[73] In addition, the network of existing private programs provides a safety valve in case of failure of the public system.

One of the most effective ways that public health issues have been addressed is through public-private partnerships that emphasize

Table 6

CMH Recommended Commitments for Improved Global Health
(billions of constant 2002 U.S. dollars)

	2001 (CMH estimates)	2007	2015
Donor Commitments			
Total Donor Commitments	7.0	27.0	38.0
Country-level programs:			
Least-Developed Countries	1.5	14.0	21.0
Other Low-Income Countries	2.0	6.0	8.0
Middle-Income Countries	2.0[a]	2.0	2.0
of which: Global Fund to Fight AIDS, Tuberculosis, and Malaria	0.0	8.0	12.0
Global Public Goods Program			
R&D	(<)0.5	3.0	4.0
of which: Global Health Research Fund	0.0	1.5	2.5
International Agencies	1.0	2.0	3.0
Domestic Resources for Health			
Least-Developed Countries	7.0	11.0	16.0
Other Low-Income Countries	43.0	62.0	74.0
Total Commitments			
Donor Commitments plus Domestic Resources	57.0	100.0	128.0

a. Donor Commitments for middle-income countries: $1.5 billion of concessional aid and $0.5 billion of nonconcessional aid.

SOURCE: WHO-CMH, *Macroeconomics and Health*, Executive Summary.

the prevention, control, and treatment of specific illnesses. Health campaigns targeted at specific at-risk groups can be especially effective when pursued through public-private partnerships of for-profit firms, non-profit organizations, domestic governments, and international agencies. Partnership initiatives involving the U.S. pharmaceutical industry from 1998-2001 have been valued at almost $2 billion.[74] Two such efforts, aimed at accelerating access to treatments for HIV/AIDS and at the elimination of river blindness, are highlighted below. (See Box, Health Public-Private Partnerships)

Non-resource issues are a less well-recognized factor affecting public health.[75] These social, political, or institutional considerations include many of the governance issues discussed in Chapter 3. Weak governmental implementation is a significant part of the problem. Corruption can divert drugs and other supplies for public health facilities to black markets. In countries where such problems exist, large-scale funding would be imprudent. In those cases, potential donors and other global leaders may need to work with local nongovernmental organizations and others to build local capacity and commitment.

Women's Health

Research by the World Bank shows that improvement of health care for women aged 15-44 offers the highest return on health care spending for any demographic group of adults.[76] In addition to the direct health benefits that accrue to the women who receive care, improvements in women's health provide multiple benefits through the various roles that women play in work, childcare, and the household. Improvement in the health, nutrition, and maternity care of women improves their ability to earn income and the health and life expectancy of their newborns, older children, and other family members.

The health data reported by developing countries, especially in Asia and Africa, show

clearly that care for women and girls is inferior to that for males. Females have higher rates of mortality, morbidity, undernourishment, and medical neglect.[77] To overcome those biases experts recommend a package of essential services for women that includes: prevention and management of unwanted pregnancies, safe pregnancy and delivery services, prevention and management of sexually transmitted diseases, promotion of positive health practices, and prevention of practices harmful to health.[78] The delivery of these services need not be expensive. Many services can be delivered at relatively low cost or through simple improvements in existing or proposed services, such as fitting services to local conditions, involving women in the design and implementation of programs, providing gender-specific information, and putting greater stress on the education of communities to change attitudes and conduct that are harmful to women.

HIV/AIDS Epidemic

AIDS has claimed over 22 million lives, three million in 2000, and orphaned more than 13 million children. More than 36 million people, over 90 percent of whom live in developing countries, are now living with HIV/AIDS. In 2000, 1.7 million people died of tuberculosis, and one million people were killed by malaria. Sub-Saharan Africa is among the worst hit regions, having 75 percent of the total HIV/AIDS population.

The Joint United Nations Program on HIV/AIDS (UNAIDS) is the main worldwide coordinating agency dedicated to combating these diseases.[†] In addition, a "Global Fund to Fight AIDS, Tuberculosis, and Malaria" was established in 2001 to attract, manage, and disburse resources in the fight against these diseases. Estimated costs of treatment world-

---

† The eight international cosponsors of UNAIDS are: The International Labor Organization; the World Bank; the World Health Organization; and the United Nations' Children's Fund, Development Program, Population Fund, Drug Control Program, and Educational Scientific and Cultural Organization.

HEALTH PUBLIC-PRIVATE PARTNERSHIPS

Efforts to improve public health services in developing countries are being enhanced through public-private partnerships that draw on the medical expertise and management experience of pharmaceutical companies. Currently, over 70 public-private partnerships in health exist, with missions ranging from research and product development to distribution and the overall strengthening of public health services. They include the Medicines for Malaria Venture (MMV), the International AIDS Vaccine Initiative (IAVI), and the Global Alliance for TB Drug Development.

The most well-known health partnerships are those that focus on the development and distribution of new drugs and vaccines to control the spread of infectious disease in developing countries. While these collaborations frequently include philanthropic donations from the private sector, the partnerships transcend the stereotype of short-term drug or vaccine donations, which are viewed as unsustainable solutions. The partnerships are created with a long-term goal of improving local health services to the point that external interventions are no longer necessary. Prominent examples of such partnerships include the Academic Alliance for AIDS Care in Africa and the international effort to combat River Blindness.

Academic Alliance for AIDS Care and Prevention in Africa — A new approach to partnership is this collaborative effort by Pfizer, leading HIV/AIDS researchers and clinicians from Africa and North America, and Makerere University in Uganda. The Alliance established the first large-scale AIDS/HIV clinic in Africa, now under construction at Makerere University, to train new medical personnel from across the continent on the latest options in treatment and prevention of HIV. The goal of the Alliance is to strengthen medical infrastructure, replicate it across Africa, and bring the latest medicines and practice techniques to bear in treating patients. The partnership also involves working with leading NGOs and carries the strong support of the Ugandan government, which has emerged as a regional leader in developing proactive strategies to prevent the spread of HIV. The partnership is unique because it specifically addresses one of the key challenges to slowing the spread of HIV infections in sub-Saharan Africa: weak health infrastructure and the absence of opportunities for advanced training and education in clinical best practices.

The MECTIZAN Donation Program in the Fight Against River Blindness — The international effort to control river blindness (onchocerciasis) is one of the most successful programs in the history of development cooperation. A painful and debilitating disease caused by a parasitic worm, river blindness is endemic in sub-Saharan Africa, parts of Latin America, and Yemen in the Middle East. Approximately 120 million are at risk, 18 million are infected, and an estimated 1 million have been blinded or severely visually impaired. The discovery of Mectizan® (ivermectin) by Merck & Co., Inc. and Merck's unprecedented decision in 1987 to donate Mectizan for as long as needed, wherever needed for the treatment of river blindness, spurred the creation of a unique multi-sectoral coalition involving Merck, the Mectizan Expert Committee, WHO, the World Bank, UNICEF, the Carter Center, dozens of national ministries of health, bilateral donors, numerous non-governmental development organizations, and many local community health workers.

Today more than 30 million patients are treated annually. The transmission of the disease has been reduced and many premature deaths have been prevented. Some 16 million children have been spared the risk of infection, more than 600,000 cases of blindness have been prevented and the disease has been virtually eliminated as a public health problem in 11 countries in West Africa alone, owing to a spraying program combined with Mectizan treatment. The achievements of the program extend beyond its immediate health benefits to socio-economic improvement, capacity building, sustainability, and strengthened health systems in infected countries. As a result of this unique public-private partnership, there is now hope that the disease can be eliminated worldwide as a public health problem and socio-economic constraint within the next decade.

SOURCES: Pfizer Inc. and Merck & Co., Inc.

wide run as high as $10 billion per year. At the end of February 2002, public and private contributions amounted to about $2 billion, of which the United States had pledged $200 million. The Bush administration has requested an additional $200 million in the 2003 budget.

Despite increased attention to the crisis of HIV/AIDS, efforts to combat the disease face many obstacles. Prevention of HIV infection is theoretically the most readily accessible and cost-effective intervention. However, effective and sustainable prevention programs require not just more education efforts but a better understanding of how to motivate individuals and communities to embrace healthier lifestyles and refrain from sexual practices, along with drug and excessive alcohol use, which increase the risk of HIV infection.

Recently, more attention has been given to care and treatment of individuals in the developing world already infected with HIV, especially with the wide availability of numerous antiretroviral drugs in North America and Europe, which have dramatically reduced the morbidity and mortality of HIV/AIDS in these regions. While the high cost of these drugs is often cited as a major barrier to increased access to HIV/AIDS drugs in resource-constrained countries, the larger issue is the lack of sufficient resources overall for most poor countries to mount a comprehensive approach to HIV prevention, care, and treatment. Access to affordable HIV medicines is but one element in addressing the needs of those infected in most developing countries.

Nevertheless, access to HIV antiretroviral drugs and other agents used to treat AIDS-associated infections and illnesses has turned attention to the role of international trade rules and intellectual property rights as they are applied in developing countries, based on an assumption that patents on pharmaceuticals are the underlying barrier to access to HIV/AIDS medicines. To this end, trade min-

isters agreed in November 2001 to the Doha Declaration of the World Trade Organization, which reiterates WTO member states' commitment to the TRIPS agreement and respects the rights of patent holders, while at the same time clarifying that countries can take action consistent with the Agreement to protect the health of their citizens. In a balanced approach that recognizes the role of intellectual property in promoting pharmaceutical innovation, the declaration recognizes that where there is a declared public health crisis, including those related to HIV/AIDS, TB, malaria or other epidemics representing a national emergency or other circumstances of extreme urgency, extraordinary measures such as compulsory licensing of patented drugs may be justified.

This clarification is a significant development. However, recent research suggests that patents and antiretroviral drugs have not been a major barrier to treatment access,[79] notwithstanding allegations to the contrary. In Africa in particular, few antiretroviral drugs are patented, and several drug manufacturers have discounted prices to their marginal cost of production or lower than cost, or have offered donations. This is also true of hundreds of essential drugs that are not under patent in Africa or other developing countries, and nonetheless are inaccessible to millions of people in ill health.

More significant barriers include a lack of political will on the part of a country's leadership, overall poor medical care and infrastructure, inefficient drug regulatory procedures, and high tariffs and taxes.[80] To sustain success and improvement to health care in the least developed and developing countries, it is important that stakeholders in the global health community focus on critically important barriers to access to medicines and services in poor countries. Little progress can be made without sustainable financing, international assistance, and additional investments in education, training, and health infrastructure and capacity in developing countries. Only progress on these fundamental issues— through partnership involving all stakeholders—will ultimately lead to better health care in least developed and developing countries.

The Role of Global Businesses in Improving Health Outcomes

As the spread of HIV/AIDS, TB, and malaria has reached crisis proportions, global businesses have recognized their stake in the crisis and have responded to it.[81] Businesses feel the effects of these diseases through the reduced ability of employees to perform their jobs, the erosion of short-term profitability, and the slowing of long-term growth. In addition, the spread of these diseases is associated with political instability and reduced security. Businesses have reacted in a variety of ways, both individually and through international organizations.

To illustrate how business are responding, we highlight two of the leading international programs that have emerged to help global companies respond to the challenges of HIV/AIDS, TB, and malaria. The Global Business Council on HIV/AIDS was established in 1997 to advocate for greater business action against the epidemic. The Council seeks to transform the business response to HIV/AIDS, making HIV/AIDS a core business issue — particularly for those companies with interests in Africa, Asia, and Latin America where the epidemic is most severe. It seeks to provide leadership on the positive impact business practice can have in fighting HIV/AIDS, by combining advocacy, policy development, and grassroots action with member companies and other stakeholders. The Council works in four key priorities areas: increased action by business, policy development and leadership, increasing business action at the national and regional levels, and changing public perceptions of the business response to HIV/AIDS.[82]

The Global Health Initiative (GHI) of the World Economic Forum was launched in 2001 to help business leaders' efforts to fight these diseases. It has focused on developing the business case for greater corporate engagement, identifying best practices in workforce and community health programs, identifying the roles of business in advocacy, and understanding options for corporate philanthropy and partnerships.[83] A GHI task force has developed a specific set of recommendations to guide business leaders. (See Box, GHI Task Force Recommendations)

GHI TASK FORCE RECOMMENDATIONS

**Companies must commit to the fight against HIV/AIDS,
TB, and malaria**

- CEOs and business leaders should make the fight against HIV/AIDS, TB, and malaria a business and policy priority for their organizations.

- CEOs and business leaders should develop a strategic vision of what impact their company individually and the private sector collectively will make, in cooperation with government and other stakeholders.

Companies should take practical steps to contribute to the prevention, care, and treatment of HIV/AIDS, TB, and malaria and towards addressing the impact of these diseases in their communities

- Companies need to begin by reviewing established workplace policy and programmes to consider practical ways to extend them in addressing the current challenges of HIV/AIDS, TB, and malaria.

- Companies should look at enhancing their relationships with local communities and at expanding activities to include developing and sharing best practices throughout their spheres of influence, actively advocating for action, and using strategic philanthropy.

- Companies should also seek opportunities to be active at the national level to support national programmes and strategies and at the global level to build greater international involvement.

- Companies should consider partnerships as being crucial to the design and implementation of policies and programmes. Governments, international organizations, community groups, academic and professional institutions, the private sector, and NGOs all bring skills and experience. Partnerships are the best way to facilitate the transfer of useful knowledge and practice.

- Companies should participate in the collective sharing of national and regional experiences in order to leverage the substantial experience that has been established.

Companies should expand their efforts to encourage others to fight against HIV/AIDS, TB, and malaria

- Advocacy is key and is needed in order to "share the load" by building a greater, broader support base. Companies should identify opportunities to advocate for increased contributions by other key stakeholders, including:

  – Other multinational and local companies so that they engage and work toward Global Goals.

  – Governments of industrialized countries so that they significantly increase their levels of official international assistance.

  – Governments of developing countries so that they fulfill their responsibility to care for their own citizens, through appropriate policies.

Companies can expand their efforts in other ways

- Companies should consider direct corporate philanthropy and partnerships as important elements in a comprehensive approach to HIV/AIDS, TB, and malaria.

- Companies should work with organizations to coordinate the private sector's response and create synergies towards achieving the global goals. Examples of such organizations include the Stop TB, Partnership, Roll Back Malaria, UNAIDS, and business organizations working against HIV/AIDS, TB, and malaria such as the Global Business Council on HIV/AIDS.

- Companies and other stakeholders should consider the significant contribution to the fight against HIV/AIDS, TB, and malaria that can flow from direct economic investment in and trade reform by developing countries.

SOURCE: World Economic Forum, *Global Health Initiative Resource Paper.*

Chapter 6

FINANCING FOR DEVELOPMENT

The resources needed to pursue the policy recommendations of the previous two chapters are much larger than those available domestically in most developing countries. Estimates of the additional external funds needed to reach the internationally agreed development goals for halving poverty, providing universal and gender-equal primary education, and achieving various health goals total $52 billion to $63 billion per year.[†] (See Table 7) Even sums at the low end of this range would approximately double the $54 billion level of development assistance from the advanced economies in 2000.

The issue of how such financial resources might be provided has risen to near the top of the international economic agenda. A summit-level United Nations conference on "Financing for Development" (FfD) took place in Monterrey, Mexico in March 2002. The final communiqué of the heads of state participating in the conference, including President George W. Bush, emphasizes many of the points made in this report. Our goals are the same: "to eradicate poverty, achieve sustained economic growth and promote sustainable development as we advance to a fully inclusive and equitable global economic system."[84] And, responsibilities are clear: "Each country has primary responsibility for its own economic and social development, and the role of national policies and development strategies cannot be overemphasized. At the same time, domestic economies are now interwoven with the global economic system and, inter alia, the effective use of trade and investment opportunities can help countries to fight poverty. National development efforts need to be supported by an enabling international environment."[85]

Conference participants recognized that for most developing countries domestic resources will be insufficient to meet development goals; external private and public resources will also be needed. The Conference noted that external private resources, especially through foreign direct investment, are a vital component of development efforts: "To attract and enhance inflows of productive capital, countries need to continue their efforts to achieve a transparent, stable and predictable investment climate, with proper contract enforcement and respect for property rights, embedded

Table 7

Estimates Of Additional Annual Costs Needed to Achieve Selected International Development Goals

Goal	Estimated Cost (billions of dollars)
Halving poverty and hunger	20
Universal and gender-equal primary education	12
International development goals for health	20-31
Total	**52-63**

SOURCES: United Nations, *Report of the High-Level Panel on Financing for Development,* June 2000, Annex and WHO, *Macroeconomics and Health,* 2001.

---

† The World Bank has estimated these costs at $40 billion to $60 billion.

48

in sound macroeconomic policies and institutions that allow businesses, both domestic and international, to operate efficiently and profitably and with maximum development impact."[86]

The heads of state also called for a substantial increase in official development assistance (ODA)[†] and other resources to complement domestic savings and private foreign investment, especially in low-income countries that are least able to attract foreign capital. The United States pledged a 50 percent increase in aid. Most important, President Bush and other national leaders recognized that the effectiveness of aid must be enhanced, both to promote development and to build greater public support for ODA programs.

A PERSPECTIVE ON OFFICIAL DEVELOPMENT ASSISTANCE

We agree in principle with the call for increased and more effective spending for development assistance. Although we have concerns about how aid has been allocated and managed in the past, a strong case for more development aid can be made on economic and humanitarian grounds and to strengthen U.S. leadership in policy engagement with developing country governments. But we see little value in spending scarce resources that have little return. Setting an arbitrary financing goal based on a percentage of GDP, as has been the practice, inverts the logic of financial decision-making. The rationale for increased development assistance must be its effectiveness, not aggregate targets.

In this regard, our views are consistent with President Bush's proposal for a new

Millennium Challenge Account within the U.S. foreign aid budget. As outlined, countries that improve governance and root out corruption, encourage economic freedom through sound economic policies, and invest in their people, would receive more aid from the United States. Increased aid of $5 billion annually, when phased-in over the next three years, would be linked to measurable improvements in performance. These new resources would be allocated to countries that undertake sound economic reforms and concentrated in areas such as health and education, where the case for support is clear because the activities are more often programmatically sound and have measurable results. CED supports this proposal and would support shifting even more of the U.S. foreign aid budget to this account and, if successful, adding more funds.

Donors should provide increases in official development assistance as long as they are confident that such aid can be spent effectively. The allocation of aid should be based on the soundness of a country's development policies and on measurable improvements in specific areas such as education and health, rather than on pre-determined country allotments. To measure the effectiveness of increased spending, more resources should be devoted to improving the collection, dissemination, and use of data on conditions in developing countries. We do not support schemes for automatic funding of aid programs through international taxes or other financing mechanisms that skirt the normal appropriations process.

Making Aid More Effective

We do not claim to have comprehensive answers to questions about how to improve the effectiveness of U.S. development assistance; a full review of the U.S. foreign assistance program is beyond the scope of this study. Nevertheless, the effectiveness of aid is a critical issue that deserves some attention

---

† ODA is defined by the Development Assistance Committee of the OECD to include financial transfers undertaken by the official sector to promote economic development and provided on concessional terms with a grant element of at least 25 percent on loans.

here. Public support for development assistance programs will only become evident when such programs demonstrate their effectiveness through measurable improvements in performance. In our view, effectiveness could be enhanced by various programmatic changes and greater emphasis on measuring outcomes. One such improvement would be to shift more resources to areas such as health and education, where the case for support is clearer because the activities are programmatically sound and the results more measurable. Another might be to make greater use of public-private partnerships. Such partnerships deploy private-sector capital, sometimes with public-sector capital, to improve public services or the management of public-sector assets.[87] Notable projects exist in which public-private partnerships have provided essential services to developing countries on a commercial basis. (See Box, Public-Private Partnership for Water and Sanitation in

Argentina) Although such partnerships have been most successful in middle- and higher-income developing countries, it may be worthwhile to explore the potential for public-private collaborations in lower-income countries, where the need is greatest.

Perhaps most important, aid should be allocated more consistently in support of states that undertake sound development policies. Research has consistently shown that development aid works best when it reinforces good policies and rewards good performers. In allocating aid, administrators should pay greater attention to the dangerous combination of fungible money and inadequate economic and political discipline, which can too easily result in aid being diverted from its intended goals, sometimes to private accounts. While aid should not be heavily laden with conditions, its allocation and disbursement should require a recipient to have policies that will ensure the aid's effectiveness.

PUBLIC-PRIVATE PARTNERSHIP FOR WATER AND SANITATION IN ARGENTINA

When the Government of Argentina signed a 30-year water and sanitation concession contract in 1993 for the Buenos Aires metropolitan area, with a population of over ten million, 2.6 million people in the area had no access to the drinking water network and five million people had no access to a waste treatment system. Ninety-five percent of the wastewater in Buenos Aires was discharged untreated into the environment.

The concession contract for Buenos Aires was awarded after a competitive bidding process to Aguas Argentinas, a consortium of international and Argentinean investors led by an affiliate of Suez Lyonnaise des Eaux. The Buenos Aires contract is the largest water services ever awarded to a private-sector company.

Since 1993, when the concession contract was awarded, Aguas Argentinas has invested over $1.6 billion in developing the needed water and sanitation facilities. This represents a yearly investment rate almost 20 times higher than the investment rate before 1993.

Aguas Argentinas has extended drinking water systems to 1.6 million new people, including 0.8 million in the poorest neighborhoods. It has connected 1 million new people to the sanitation network. It has increased drinking water production capacity by 37 percent, ending summertime water shortages. And all this has been done with a lower price of water in 2001 than in 1993.

Between now and the expiration of the concession in 2023, the consortium is contractually bound to extend drinking water service to the entire population of Buenos Aires and to provide wastewater treatment services to 95 percent of the population (from the pre-concession level of 50 percent and the current level of 60 percent).

Such policies include those we have empha-sized throughout this report: honest govern-ment, reliable and transparent accounting, and other appropriate economic, political, and social policies. Even if the volume of aid is low, allocations requiring sound polices allow donor countries to support local efforts and maintain a dialogue with the recipient on how best to improve those policies.

The communiqué of the Financing for Development Conference calls on developed countries to make concrete efforts toward the 30-year old target of providing 0.7 percent of gross national product for ODA. The OECD countries as a group currently provide about 0.3 percent of GNP, and the United States 0.1 percent. It further calls for a study of "innova-tive sources of finance," including the use of Special Drawing Right (SDR)[†] allocations of the International Monetary Fund for develop-ment purposes.

How public resources from the more eco-nomically advanced countries might be gener-ated to meet the international development goals is very controversial. Proposals for such "innovative" sources of financing have not been lacking. United Kingdom Chancellor of the Exchequer Gordon Brown and DaimlerChrysler Chairman Jurgen Schrempp, among others, have made prominent calls for a new Marshall Plan.[88] Finance ministers of the European Union have asked for a formal examination of how taxes on foreign currency transactions, carbon dioxide, or arms sales might be used to finance development goals.[89] George Soros has proposed that the IMF issue new SDRs for international financial assis-tance; in Soros's proposal, the IMF would dis-tribute to all its members a one-time issue of SDRs equal to about $27.5 billion.[90] The rich-

est IMF members, who would receive most of the SDR allocation, would donate their shares (estimated to be nearly $18 billion) for inter-national assistance.

Other innovative proposals focus primari-ly on the form of aid and its means of delivery. The U.S. International Financial Institution Advisory Commission (the Meltzer Commission), for example, recommended the conversion of World Bank aid from loans to grants. Some have suggested that bilateral donors could improve the efficiency of aid giving by creating a "common pool," and some advocates have suggested ways to extend the scope of debt relief offered through the HIPC initiative, beyond that described above.

Such proposals for "innovative transfers" have been discussed as theoretical concepts for decades. Yet issues about their practicality and their ultimate consequences remain unresolved. Who would be accountable for such funds? How could donors be assured that funds would be used for intended pur-poses? What authorities would impose an international tax? What criteria would be used for the disbursement of funds? How would transparency be ensured?

The proposal for an international tax on foreign currency transactions illustrates some of these problems. Implementation would require either the creation of an international authority to collect the tax, an unrealistic and unappealing option, or that every national government impose an identical tax. The lat-ter appears most unlikely, since countries that promote themselves as "tax havens" would be unlikely to participate. Moreover, while such a tax may make sense for an individual country, to regulate the term structure of its debt, it would seem anomalous to tax international capital movements that promote develop-ment. Such a tax, if effective, would lessen the resources available to developing countries. Creating an automatic stream of funds might also put pressure on fund managers to spend

---

† Special Drawing Rights are an international reserve asset cre-ated by the International Monetary Fund in 1969. SDRs serve as a unit of account and means of payment among IMF members. The value of an SDR is determined by the weight-ed values of the major international currencies, the dollar, euro, yen, and pound.

the money in ways that might not always be prudent.

Similarly, issuing SDRs for development offers the appeal of "free" money. However, that is an illusion that creates its own problems. Although a new SDR allocation would create new money, the resources that are transferred are not free and the additional demand would pose the danger of additional inflation. Giving an international institution the right to create new money would set a bad precedent since it could open the floodgates to global inflation. Whether to add to the money supply is typically a decision left to national authorities. Another supposed virtue is that an SDR allocation might be made without explicitly taxing citizens of developed countries and with little public scrutiny. But the transfer of SDRs would be the same as a transfer of real resources, and thus would be equivalent to a real tax. In our view development aid should compete in national budgets against other needs; it should be transparent and not hidden behind a complex financial transaction.

The Marshall Plan and Foreign Aid

Since the end of World War II, the United States has provided assistance of various kinds and for various purposes to other countries. The effort began with the Marshall Plan, which assisted in the post-war recovery of the European economies. The success of the Marshall Plan has made it a symbol for leadership in the international economic system. (See Box, The Marshall Plan) Following the recovery of Europe, the United States began directing financial and food aid to newly independent states and developing countries in Africa, Asia, and Latin America.

The Marshall Plan had two prominent features: the expenditure of a large amount of money and the political acceptance of the idea that it was important for the United

---

THE MARSHALL PLAN

Two years after the Allied victory in World War II, many Europeans faced widespread hunger, unemployment, and housing shortages. The general economic dislocation and physical destruction of the war threatened a breakdown of commercial, political, and social conditions. In that atmosphere, Secretary of State George C. Marshall proposed a bold plan for European reconstruction with financial aid from the United States. Ultimately, the Marshall Plan would transfer about one percent of U.S. GNP to European countries annually over the span of four years and be successful in helping to revive the European economies.

The success of the plan has made it a symbol for leadership in the international economic arena. In the more than 50 years since Marshall's call for action, other leaders have seen similar pressing needs and echoed the call for a "new Marshall Plan." Some leaders again are using the Marshall Plan as a reference as they call for the rebuilding of Afghanistan and the financing of international development goals.

The money spent during the period from 1948 to 1951 provided scarce foreign exchange to acquire additional resources to economies that had in place the other human, political, and social requirements for reconstruction and recovery. Even much of the economic infrastructure—electricity, rail, roads, and water —had already been rebuilt. From an operational perspective, the United States was able to give money to well-functioning governments to use according to their own priorities. The conditions existing in today's developing countries are much different and more complex. Most lack the human and physical resources that existed in Europe; political and financial institutions are generally not as strong. It is as questionable whether they could effectively absorb such large sums of money as whether the American people would be prepared to make such an economic sacrifice.

States to act as an international leader. It is the second feature that is most relevant in today's environment. Key to Marshall's success was his ability to motivate and involve business and political leaders who had formerly been more isolationist in their outlook. A group of American business leaders, in particular Paul Hoffman and other founders of the Committee for Economic Development, played a significant role in mobilizing public and business support for the plan. Hoffman, a visionary business and political leader, became head of the Economic Cooperation Administration, which administered the Marshall Plan. Marshall was also able to unite both political parties behind his understanding that American prosperity depended on our willingness to help others to achieve economic development. Then, as now, the parties and the public were deeply divided over the role the United States should play in the international arena. It is predominantly in the exercise of leadership that the Marshall Plan provides a reference point for today.

In 2000, the United States provided some form of bilateral foreign assistance to over 140 countries. More than 75 percent of the aid, however, was concentrated in the top ten recipients, lead by Israel and Egypt. Most of that aid was for security rather than development purposes. Whereas the Marshall Plan channeled an average of about 1 percent of U.S. GNP to recipient countries, that figure now stands at about 0.1 percent for official development assistance. ODA, however, is only a small portion of the public resources provided by the United States to maintain a secure and stable international order. International order and security, including the containment of terrorism, is (however unfortunately) a necessary condition for global development in today's world. In practice, a high degree of specialization has emerged among the developed countries in the provision of international public goods; the U.S. has allocated its resources primarily to security, whereas our European and Japanese allies have specialized in development aid.

Foreign aid today is provided in a variety of ways and for a variety of purposes. For example development aid is provided on a multilateral basis through the World Bank and regional development banks and bilaterally through USAID. The United States also provides humanitarian food aid, debt forgiveness through bilateral and multilateral programs, and aid for political and national security purposes. Although not classified as "official aid," commercial credits for foreign purchases of U.S. goods and services and political risk insurance for investments are among the economic programs available to help developing countries. The United States also provides funds to the IMF to finance short-term balance of payments crises, which are now used exclusively by developing and transitional countries.

In the war against terrorism, the United States can be expected to maintain or expand funding for security assistance, which aims to stabilize countries and regions where our security interests are paramount. Where we provide such assistance, we should not also expect it to be very effective in support of development goals. Experience has shown that when security concerns are the primary determinant of funding allocations, economic development goals are unlikely to be met simultaneously. In a great many cases, the countries that receive security assistance pursue inappropriate economic policies but have little incentive to improve them since the aid is not contingent on performance.

It is reasonable to expect that humanitarian aid, as distinct from development aid, will also increase. The American people have a history of supporting humanitarian causes, especially when made conscious of dire need caused by war, drought, and famine. Such assistance is likely to be needed at heightened levels as the war on terrorism continues.

Although we face fundamentally different circumstances today than those faced by Marshall, the challenge is similar in this respect: How can the urgency of the problems facing developing countries be articulated in a way that makes it clear to those in the advanced economies that it is in their interests to help craft a solution to those problems? And, how can we ensure that the resources spent in the cause of poverty reduction reach their intended goal most efficiently and effectively?

As those questions are debated, we believe it is important to keep development aid in perspective. The most effective way for a government to finance development is through making the policy changes that allow the country to attract private resources. In recent years the resources available through private financing for trade and investment have vastly outstripped those available through development assistance agencies. In 1999, net ODA from the advanced countries was about one-quarter the amount of FDI of $208 billion to developing countries.[91] Moreover, worldwide FDI flows of nearly $900 billion indicate that the potential flow of funds to developing countries is much greater. Experience shows that private financing through foreign direct investment and loans will flow to countries that have the rule of law, non-corrupt governments, and appropriate economic policies. Countries such as Brazil, Korea, and Mexico have for the most part graduated from development aid to private funding in world financial markets. The recommendations of this report are designed to help extend the flow of private resources to other developing countries.

Official development aid can be critical for the least developed economies, but for many countries it is not the most important source of external funds. For countries that are pursuing intelligent development policies, financial assistance through one of the multilateral development banks or bilateral aid donors can be of significant help. Until they can achieve sustained economic growth, many countries will remain dependent on development aid to augment their relative lack of human, financial, and physical resources. In addition, there are exceptional situations when aid can play a vital role, such as when a democratically elected government replaces a corrupt and authoritarian one and inherits a critical economic situation. In such circumstances, aid can help to secure economic stability, especially if it is allocated to counter-corruption programs and other programs where evidence can be secured to measure improvements in performance.

CONCLUSION

Global economic development since the end of World War II has been remarkable: the persistence of poverty throughout the developing world should not obscure that fact. In the developing countries as a whole per capita GDP has tripled since 1950, life expectancy has increased by nearly 50 percent, and infant mortality has fallen from about 180 per 1000 births to under 60, although progress has been uneven. Among the factors that led to these successes have been an increased reliance on markets to allocate resources, increased foreign trade and private investment, public investments in agricultural research underpinning the "Green Revolution" that changed the nature of food production, and publicly financed development projects ranging from the building of basic infrastructure to the distribution of food and medicines to meet basic human needs.

Economic development is a complex process. There is no patented formula for success. For development to occur, governments, businesses, civic organizations, and individuals must make sound decisions that promote economic growth within the context of their unique circumstances.

Each nation is responsible for its own economic, political, and social development. That point cannot be overstressed. The role of government leadership is vitally important. Policy choices made by developing country governments to a great extent create the environment for economic growth or stagnation. All developing countries face virtually identical external circumstances with regard to opportunities to export goods and services and to import technologies and financial support. Other than conditions dictated by location or natural resources, which cannot be changed, the distinguishing feature that sets nations apart economically is their choice of policies to stimulate economic growth, invest in people, and attack poverty.

The United States and other advanced economies have an important role to play as well. The developed nations must maintain global economic and political stability, establishing an environment in which developing countries can thrive if they make sound policy choices. They must also provide the necessary political and financial support to help developing countries carry through on the policy choices they make.

Financial support flows through trade, investment, and development aid. Of these, trade and investment are the most important. Perhaps of greatest benefit to the world's most impoverished would be for the U.S. government and our OECD partners to establish trade policies that are more open. Ideally, these policies would completely eliminate trade barriers and production subsidies that hinder developing country exports. The effort could start by speeding up the elimination of tariffs under the Agreement on Textiles and Clothing. In the area of investment, we would press for a multilateral investment code and provide greater support for anti-corruption measures and other policies

that would help developing countries to improve their investment climates.

Debate over numeric targets for official (government) aid, which has dominated political debate, is a distraction from the more significant sources of financial and non-financial forms of support, which come from the private sector. Given the relative sizes of financial flows, aid is not the most important conduit for helping developing countries, although for the least developed it can be a critical resource. In foreign aid, we would not hesitate to spend any dollar that can be spent effectively and efficiently; and there is room to increase aid now.

Global businesses and their leaders have pivotal roles to play in various dimensions of the poverty problem. In developing countries, they demonstrate new technologies, provide employment and often raise employment practices by providing education and health benefits, and lend political support to critical policy reforms. In many places, socially responsible MNCs contribute substantially to the betterment of the communities and nations in which they operate. In developed countries, business leaders should be taking an active role in support of multilateral programs that advance economic development and global poverty reduction, including the appropriate expansion of effective foreign aid.

In summary, policies that promote economic growth are a prerequisite for the reduction of poverty. These policies include market-oriented solutions to economic problems, openness to foreign trade and investment, and funding to improve education and health. A nation that is poor will not become rich over night, but it can begin to solve its economic problems by putting the right policies in place. Seemingly small annual increments to income growth cumulate into large changes in a country's standard of living over a generation and greatly reduce the number of people living in dire poverty.

Those of us who live in nations that have achieved a high level of economic prosperity must do what we can to see that other nations have the opportunity to enjoy a similar standard of living. It is in our economic, political, and humanitarian interests to foster a more prosperous, democratic, and stable world. As advances in communication and transportation shrink the distances between global haves and have-nots, we must act on the understanding that we truly share a common future. Economic integration through trade and investment, supported by sound domestic policies that build human capabilities, is a positive-sum strategy. It has the potential to raise the standard of living for all participants and to make our shared future brighter, more secure, and more prosperous.

ENDNOTES

1. Commission on U.S. National Security in the 21st Century, *Phase II Report on a U.S. National Security Strategy for the 21st Century* (April 2000), p. 7, available at <www.nssg.gov/PhaseII.pdf>.

2. George W. Bush, "Remarks by the President on Global Development at the Inter-American Development Bank," (White House Press Release, Washington, DC, March 14, 2002).

3. Peter H. Lindert and Jeffrey G. Williamson, *Does Globalization Make the World More Unequal?*, Working Paper no. 8228 (Cambridge, MA: National Bureau of Economic Research, 2001), and David Dollar and Aart Kraay, *Growth is Good for the Poor*, Working Paper Series 2587 (Washington, DC: World Bank, 2000).

4. David Dollar, *Globalization, Inequality, and Poverty since 1980*, (working paper, World Bank, November 2001), p. 2, available at <econ.worldbank.org/files/2944_globalization-inequality-and-poverty.pdf>.

5. Dollar, *Globalization, Inequality, and Poverty since 1980*, p. 2

6. Amartya Sen, *Development as Freedom* (New York, NY: Anchor Books, 1999), p. 20.

7. Dani Rodrik, "The New Global Economy and Developing Countries: Making Openness Work," *Overseas Development Council Policy Essay*, no. 24 (1999).

8. Angus Maddison, "The Millennium — Poor Until 1820," *Wall Street Journal*, January 11, 1999, p. R54.

9. World Bank, *World Development Indicators 2001* (Washington, D.C.: World Bank, 2001), table 1.4.

10. World Bank, *World Development Report 2000/2001: Attacking Poverty* (New York, NY: Oxford University Press, 2000), pp. 16-21.

11. United Nations Educational, Scientific and Cultural Organization (UNESCO), *Education for All 2000 Assessment: Statistical Document* (2000), Executive Summary, p. 8.

12. World Bank, "2001 Poverty Update," *World Bank Issue Briefs* (September 2001).

13. Organization for Economic Co-operation and Development (OECD), *A Better World For All*, p. 20.

14. OECD, *A Better World For All* (2000), pp. 12-15, available at <www.paris21.org/betterworld> and OECD, "Maternal Morality: Helping Mothers Live," *OECD Observer*, no. 223 (December 2000).

15. Joint United Nations Programme on HIV/AIDS (UNAIDS) and World Health Organization (WHO), *Epidemic Update: December 2001* (Geneva: UNAIDS, 2001), p. 29.

16. World Bank, "Development Goals," available at <www.developmentgoals.org>.

17. Corporate Council on Africa, "About CCA," available at <www.africacncl.org/about/index.htm>.

18. World Bank, *World Development Indicators Database*, available at <https://publications.worldbank.org/subscriptions/WDI/>.

19. World Bank, "Income Poverty: Prospects for poverty reduction: Scenarios for the next fifteen years," *Data on Poverty*, available at <www.worldbank.org/poverty/data/trends/scenario.htm> .

20. University of Maryland, Program on International Policy Attitudes, "Americans on Foreign Aid and World Hunger: A Study of U.S. Public Attitudes," February 2, 2001, available at <www.pipa.org/OnlineReports/BFW/toc.html>.

21. Michael B. Gerrard, "Public-Private Partnerships," *Finance and Development*, vol. 38, no. 3 (2001).

22. World Bank, *World Development Report 2002: Building Institutions for Markets* (New York, NY: Oxford University Press, 2001), p. iii.

23. Sen, *Development as Freedom*, p. 16.

24. Sen, *Development as Freedom*, pp. 15-17, 149-151.

25. Hernando de Soto, *The Mystery of Capital: Why Capitalism Triumphs in the West and Fails Everywhere Else* (New York, NY: Basic Books, 2000).

26. Erick Rabemananoro, "MicroStart Makes a Difference," *Choices Magazine*, vol. 11, no. 1 (2002), pp. 12-13.

27. See for example, Committee for Economic Development, *Improving Global Financial Stability*, (New York, NY: CED, 2000), p. 16.

28. World Bank, *World Development Report 2002*, p. 105

29. Robin Emmott, "Mexico Bribery 'Widespread'," *Financial Times*, October 31, 2001.

30. OECD, "The fight against bribery and corruption," *OECD Policy Brief* (September 2000).

31. Global Reporting Initiative, "GRI Overview," available at <www.globalreporting.org>.

32. Thomas F. Rutherford and David G. Tarr, *Trade Liberalization and Endogenous Growth in a Small Open Economy: A Quantitative Assessment*, Working Paper Series 1970 (Washington, DC: World Bank, 1998). Also, see World Bank, *World Development Report 2000/2001*, p. 63.

33. Helmut Reisen and Marcelo Soto, "Which Types of Capital Inflows Foster Developing-Country Growth?" *International Finance*, vol. 4, no. 1 (2001), p. 10.

34. World Bank, *Global Development Finance 2001* (Washington, DC: World Bank, 2000), p. 36.

35. World Bank, *Global Development Finance 2001*, p. 38.

36. United Nations Conference on Trade and Development (UNCTAD), *World Investment Report 2001* (New York, NY: United Nations, 2001), chapter 1.

37. E. Borensztein, J. De Gregorio and J.W. Lee, " How Does Foreign Direct Investment Affect Economic Growth?" *Journal of International Economics*, vol. 45, no. 1 (1998), pp. 115-135, as cited in Linda Lim, *The Globalization Debate: Issues and Challenges* (Geneva: International Labor Office, 2001), p. 19.

38. Guy Pfeffermann, "Poverty Reduction in Developing Countries: The Role of Private Enterprise," *Finance and Development*, vol. 38, no. 2 (2001).

39. World Trade Organization, *Doha Ministerial Declaration* (Doha, Qatar, November 14, 2001), paragraph 20.

40. International Textiles and Clothing Bureau, *Agreement on Textiles and Clothing: Evaluation of Implementation*, August 3, 1999, p. 1, available at <www.itcb.org/Documents/itcb-mi3.pdf>.

41. World Bank, *World Development Indicators 2001*, table 4.6.

42. World Bank, *Global Economic Prospects and the Developing Countries 2002: Making Trade Work for the World's Poor* (Washington, DC: World Bank, 2001), pp. 166-168.

43. Oxfam International, *Eight Broken Promises: Why the WTO Isn't Working for the World's Poor*, Oxfam Briefing Paper 9 (2001), p. 5.

44. World Bank, *Global Economic Prospects 2002*, p. xv.

45. International Textiles and Clothing Bureau, *Agreement on Textiles and Clothing*, p. 8.

46. Committee for Economic Development, *Breaking New Ground in U.S. Trade Policy* (New York, NY: CED, 1991) and Committee for Economic Development, *U.S. Trade Policy Beyond the Uruguay Round* (New York, NY: CED, 1994).

47. U.S. Congressional Budget Office, *Antidumping Action in the United States and Around the World: An Update* (Washington, DC: CBO, June 2001), p. xi.

48. Committee for Economic Development, *American Workers and Economic Change* (New York, NY: CED, 1996).

49. Committee for Economic Development, *From Protest to Progress: Addressing Labor and Environmental Conditions Through Freer Trade* (New York, NY: CED, 2001).

50. Sen, *Development as Freedom*, pp. 87-110.

51. Sen, *Development as Freedom*, p. 89.

52. Committee for Economic Development, *Improving Global Financial Stability*, pp. 24-25.

53. International Monetary Fund and International Development Association, *Tracking of Poverty-Reducing Public Spending in Heavily Indebted Poor Countries (HIPCs)*, (working paper, IMF, March 2001), p. 6.

54. OECD Development Assistance Committee, *Shaping the 21st Century: The Contribution of Development Co-operation* (Paris: OECD, 1996), p. 10.

55. Ramon Lopez, Vinod Thomas, and Yan Wang, *Addressing the Education Puzzle: The Distribution of Education and Economic Reforms*, Working Paper Series 2031(Washington, DC: World Bank, 1998), p. 9.

56. Gene Sperling, "Educating the World," *New York Times*, November 22, 2001.

57. OECD, *A Better World For All*, p. 8.

58. World Education Forum, "Who Pays for Education?" (press release, Dakar, Senegal, April 26, 2000).

59. OECD Development Assistance Committee, "Development Cooperation: 2000 Report" *DAC Journal*, vol. 2, no. 1 (2001), p. 154.

60. UNESCO, *The Global Initiative towards Education for All: A Framework for Mutual Understanding*, UNESCO Education Sector Working Document (2001), p. 8.

61. World Bank, *Engendering Development: Through Gender Equality in Rights, Resources, and Voice* (Washington, D.C.: World Bank, 2001), p. 11.

62. World Bank, "Harness The Power of Education for All," (World Bank Press Release, Washington, DC, April 27, 2001).

63. OECD, *A Better World For All*, p. 9.

64. World Education Forum, *The Dakar Framework for Action* (Dakar, Senegal, April 28, 2000), foreword.

65. Committee for Economic Development, *The Digital Economy: Promoting Competition, Innovation, and Opportunity* (New York, NY: CED, 2001).

66. John Strauss and Duncan Thomas, "Health, Nutrition, and Economic Development," *Journal of Economic Literature*, vol. XXXVI, no. 2 (1998), pp. 766-817.

67. WHO, *World Health Report 2001* (Geneva: WHO, 2001), annex table 2, p. 144.

68. World Bank, "Health, Nutrition, and Population Sector Strategy," *World Bank Health, Nutrition, and Population Series*, September 1997, p. ix.

69. WHO Commission on Macroeconomics and Health, *Macroeconomics and Health: Investing in Health for Economic Development*, (Geneva: WHO, 2001).

70. WHO CMH, *Macroeconomics and Health*, p. 1.

71. WHO CMH, *Macroeconomics and Health*, p. 2.

72. WHO CMH, *Macroeconomics and Health*, p. 7.

73. Deon Filmer, Jeffrey Hammer, and Lant Pritchett, *Health Policy in Poor Countries: Weak Links in the Chain*, Working Paper Series 1874 (Washington, DC: World Bank, 1997), p. 27.

74. Pharmaceutical Research and Manufactures of America, "WTO Doha Declaration Reaffirms Value of Intellectual Property Protection," (PHARMA Press Release, November 14, 2001).

75. Filmer, Hammer, and Pritchett, *Health Policy in Poor Countries*.

76. World Bank, "A New Agenda for Women's Health and Nutrition," available at <www.worldbank.org/html/extdr/hnp/health/newagenda/women.htm>.

77. Sen, *Development as Freedom*, chapter 8.

78. World Bank, "A New Agenda for Women's Health and Nutrition."

79. Amir Attaran and Lee Gillespie-White, "Do Patents for Antiretroviral Drugs Constrain Access to AIDS Treatment in Africa?," *Journal of the American Medical Association (JAMA)*, vol. 286, no. 15 (2001), p. 1886.

80. Attaran and Gillespie-White, "Do Patents for Antiretroviral Drugs Constrain Access to AIDS Treatment in Africa?," p. 1886.

81. World Economic Forum, "Global Health Initiative," *WEF Resource Paper* (February 2002).

82. The Global Business Council on HIV/AIDS, "What We Do," available at <http://www.businessfightsaids.org/index.html>.

83. World Economic Forum, "Global Health Initiative."

84. United Nations, *Monterrey Consensus: Draft Outcome of the International Conference on Financing for Development* (Monterrey, Mexico, March 22, 2002), paragraph 1.

85. United Nations, *Monterrey Consensus: Draft Outcome of the International Conference on Financing for Development*, paragraph 6.

86. United Nations, *Monterrey Consensus: Draft Outcome of the International Conference on Financing for Development*, paragraph 21.

87. Gerrard, "Public-Private Partnerships."

88. Chancellor of the Exchequer Gordon Brown, "Speech to the Federal Reserve Bank of New York," (Speech, New York, NY, November 16, 2001) and Frank Swoboda, "Carmaker Shares Global Vision: DaimlerChrysler Chief Wants a 'Marshall Plan'," *Washington Post*, November 30, 2001, p. E3.

89. Gordon Brown, "Speech to the Federal Reserve Bank of New York."

90. George Soros, *Draft Report on Globalization* (New York, NY: Public Affairs, 2001), p. 7.

91. UNCTAD, *World Investment Report 2000* (New York, NY: United Nations, 2000), pp. 5-7.

MEMORANDA OF COMMENT, RESERVATION, OR DISSENT

Page 4, THOMAS J. BUCKHOLTZ

Businesses, governments, and other institutions should strive to simplify the rules of society, so that all people can participate as actively and broadly as they desire to in the global economy and society as a whole.

Page 4, THOMAS J. BUCKHOLTZ

Additional avenues for promoting economic growth and reducing poverty include grassroots and interpersonal interactions. People throughout the world gain opportunities to enrich each other's lives. Businesses and governments should take direct and indirect steps to foster international discourse among individuals and between people and institutions.

Page 5, PETER A. BENOLIEL with which JOSH S. WESTON has asked to be associated.

Mention should be made of the U.S. Administration's recent implementation of tariffs on imported steel. While primarily targeted at steel exports of the more advanced economies, it belies and compromises the U.S. leadership in promoting the reduction of trade barriers. It will also have the net effect of reducing steel exports from less developed countries as well as a negative impact upon smaller domestic producers utilizing steel in their products.

Not unexpectedly, retaliatory trade sanctions are imminent at the hands of the European Commission. The growing presence of trade barriers can have only a negative effect upon less developed economies.

Page 5, PETER A. BENOLIEL with which JOSH S. WESTON has asked to be associated.

A most important recommendation, which the U.S. Administration eschewed in favor of higher tariffs on steel!

Page 25, ALAN BELZER with which JOSH S. WESTON has asked to be associated.

Overall, I am in agreement with the report with one major reservation, which concerns the lowering of barriers to imports by developing countries. The report states as follows:

Developing countries have much to gain from lowering barriers to imports. Except in rare cases, for example when there are very large economies of scale, the protection of domestic industries serves only to raise the costs of goods and services and distort the allocation of domestic resources.

The foregoing greatly understates the need for protection of fledgling industries in developing countries. The best models of developing countries that have had significant economic growth are Japan, Korea, and Taiwan, all of which protected their fledgling industries. On the other hand, Argentina, a small but somewhat developed country has caused havoc in its economy by a number of actions, the most notable being that of opening up to foreign competition too quickly.

OBJECTIVES OF THE COMMITTEE FOR ECONOMIC DEVELOPMENT

For 60 years, the Committee for Economic Development has been a respected influence on the formation of business and public policy. CED is devoted to these two objectives:

To develop, through objective research and informed discussion, findings and recommendations for private and public policy that will contribute to preserving and strengthening our free society, achieving steady economic growth at high employment and reasonably stable prices, increasing productivity and living standards, providing greater and more equal opportunity for every citizen, and improving the quality of life for all.

To bring about increasing understanding by present and future leaders in business, government, and education, and among concerned citizens, of the importance of these objectives and the ways in which they can be achieved.

CED's work is supported by private voluntary contributions from business and industry, foundations, and individuals. It is independent, nonprofit, nonpartisan, and nonpolitical.

Through this business-academic partnership, CED endeavors to develop policy statements and other research materials that commend themselves as guides to public and business policy; that can be used as texts in college economics and political science courses and in management training courses; that will be considered and discussed by newspaper and magazine editors, columnists, and commentators; and that are distributed abroad to promote better understanding of the American economic system.

CED believes that by enabling business leaders to demonstrate constructively their concern for the general welfare, it is helping business to earn and maintain the national and community respect essential to the successful functioning of the free enterprise capitalist system.

CED PROFESSIONAL AND ADMINISTRATIVE STAFF

CHARLES E.M. KOLB
President

STATEMENTS ON NATIONAL POLICY ISSUED BY THE COMMITTEE FOR ECONOMIC DEVELOPMENT

SELECTED PUBLICATIONS:

A New Vision for Health Care: A Leadership Role for Business *(2002)*

Preschool For All: Investing In a Productive and Just Society *(2002)*

From Protest to Progress: Addressing Labor and Environmental Conditions Through Freer Trade *(2001)*

The Digital Economy: Promoting Competition, Innovation, and Opportunity *(2001)*

Reforming Immigration: Helping Meet America's Need for a Skilled Workforce *(2001)*

Measuring What Matters: Using Assessment and Accountability to Improve Student Learning *(2001)*

Improving Global Financial Stability *(2000)*

The Case for Permanent Normal Trade Relations with China *(2000)*

Welfare Reform and Beyond: Making Work Work *(2000)*

Breaking the Litigation Habit: Economic Incentives for Legal Reform *(2000)*

New Opportunities for Older Workers *(1999)*

Investing in the People's Business: A Business Proposal for Campaign Finance Reform *(1999)*

The Employer's Role in Linking School and Work *(1998)*

Employer Roles in Linking School and Work: Lessons from Four Urban Communities *(1998)*

America's Basic Research: Prosperity Through Discovery *(1998)*

Modernizing Government Regulation: The Need For Action *(1998)*

U.S. Economic Policy Toward The Asia-Pacific Region *(1997)*

Connecting Inner-City Youth To The World of Work *(1997)*

Fixing Social Security *(1997)*

Growth With Opportunity *(1997)*

American Workers and Economic Change *(1996)*

Connecting Students to a Changing World: A Technology Strategy for Improving Mathematics and Science Education *(1995)*

Cut Spending First: Tax Cuts Should Be Deferred to Ensure a Balanced Budget *(1995)*

Rebuilding Inner-City Communities: A New Approach to the Nation's Urban Crisis *(1995)*

Who Will Pay For Your Retirement? The Looming Crisis *(1995)*

Putting Learning First: Governing and Managing the Schools for High Achievement *(1994)*

Prescription for Progress: The Uruguay Round in the New Global Economy *(1994)*

*From Promise to Progress: Towards a New Stage in U.S.-Japan Economic Relations *(1994)*

U.S. Trade Policy Beyond The Uruguay Round *(1994)*

In Our Best Interest: NAFTA and the New American Economy *(1993)*

What Price Clean Air? A Market Approach to Energy and Environmental Policy *(1993)*

Why Child Care Matters: Preparing Young Children For A More Productive America *(1993)*

Restoring Prosperity: Budget Choices for Economic Growth *(1992)*

The United States in the New Global Economy: A Rallier of Nations *(1992)*

The Economy and National Defense: Adjusting to Cutbacks in the Post-Cold War Era *(1991)*

Politics, Tax Cuts and the Peace Dividend *(1991)*

The Unfinished Agenda: A New Vision for Child Development and Education *(1991)*

*Statements issued in association with CED counterpart organizations in foreign countries.

Foreign Investment in the United States: What Does It Signal? *(1990)*

An America That Works: The Life-Cycle Approach to a Competitive Work Force *(1990)*

Breaking New Ground in U.S. Trade Policy *(1990)*

Battling America's Budget Deficits *(1989)*

*Strengthening U.S.-Japan Economic Relations *(1989)*

Who Should Be Liable? A Guide to Policy for Dealing with Risk *(1989)*

Investing in America's Future: Challenges and Opportunities for Public Sector Economic Policies *(1988)*

Children in Need: Investment Strategies for the Educationally Disadvantaged *(1987)*

Finance and Third World Economic Growth *(1987)*

Reforming Health Care: A Market Prescription *(1987)*

Work and Change: Labor Market Adjustment Policies in a Competitive World *(1987)*

Leadership for Dynamic State Economies *(1986)*

Investing in Our Children: Business and the Public Schools *(1985)*

Fighting Federal Deficits: The Time for Hard Choices *(1985)*

Strategy for U.S. Industrial Competitiveness *(1984)*

Productivity Policy: Key to the Nation's Economic Future *(1983)*

Energy Prices and Public Policy *(1982)*

Public Private Partnership: An Opportunity for Urban Communities *(1982)*

Reforming Retirement Policies *(1981)*

Transnational Corporations and Developing Countries: New Policies for a Changing World Economy *(1981)*

Stimulating Technological Progress *(1980)*

Redefining Government's Role in the Market System *(1979)*

Jobs for the Hard to Employ: New Directions for a Public-Private Partnership *(1978)*

CED COUNTERPART ORGANIZATIONS

Close relations exist between the Committee for Economic Development and independent, nonpolitical research organizations in other countries. Such counterpart groups are composed of business executives and scholars and have objectives similar to those of CED, which they pursue by similarly objective methods. CED cooperates with these organizations on research and study projects of common interest to the various countries concerned. This program has resulted in a number of joint policy statements involving such international matters as energy, East-West trade, assistance to developing countries, and the reduction of nontariff barriers to trade.

CE	Circulo de Empresarios Madrid, Spain
CEAL	Consejo Empresario de America Latina Buenos Aires, Argentina
CEDA	Committee for Economic Development of Australia Sydney, Australia
EVA	Centre for Finnish Business and Policy Studies Helsinki, Finland
FAE	Forum de Administradores de Empresas Lisbon, Portugal
FDE	Belgian Enterprise Foundation Brussels, Belgium
IDEP	Institut de l'Entreprise Paris, France
IW	Institut der deutschen Wirtschaft Koeln Cologne, Germany
経済同友会	Keizai Doyukai Tokyo, Japan
SMO	Stichting Maatschappij en Onderneming The Netherlands
SNS	Studieförbundet Naringsliv och Samhälle Stockholm, Sweden